OLD MOORE'S

HOROSCOPE AND ASTRAL DIARY

ARIES

foulsham
LONDON • NEW YORK • TORONTO • SYDNEY

foulsham

The Publishing House, Bennetts Close,
Cippenham, Slough, Berks SL1 5AP

ISBN 0-572-02984-5

Printed in Great Britain by Cox & Wyman Ltd, Reading, Berkshire.

CONTENTS

INTRODUCTION

Another year rolls around, and devotees of astrology are keen to know what the trends for the coming period might be. For many centuries Old Moore has been casting his gaze heavenward, to mark the passage of the planets through the zodiac and interpret their meanings for those of us here on the Earth. He continues this quest throughout the year of 2005.

The Astral Diaries have been specifically created to allow you to get the most from astrological patterns and the way they have a bearing on not only your zodiac sign, but nuances within it. Using the diary section of the book you can read about the influences and possibilities of each and every day of the year. It will be possible for you to see when you are likely to be cheerful and happy or those times when your nature is in retreat and you will be more circumspect. There is a space on the diary pages for notes of your own, and the diary will help to give you a feel for the specific 'cycles' of astrology and the way they can subtly change your day-to-day life. For example, when you see the sign ☿, this means that the planet Mercury is retrograde at that time. Retrograde means it appears to be running backwards through the zodiac. Such a happening has a significant effect on communication skills, but this is only one small aspect of how the Astral Diary can help you.

With the Astral Diary the story doesn't end with the diary pages. Old Moore has established simple ways for you to work out the zodiac sign the Moon occupied at the time of your birth, and what this means for your personality. In addition, if you know the time of day you were born, it is possible to discover your Ascendant, yet another important guide to your personal make-up and potential.

Many readers are interested in relationships and in knowing how well they get on with people of other astrological signs. You might also be interested in the way you appear to very different sorts of individuals. If you are such a person, the section on Venus will be of particular interest. Despite the rapidly changing position of this planet, Old Moore has made it possible for you to work out your Venus sign, and to learn what bearing it will have on your life.

Using the Astral Diaries you can travel with Old Moore on one of the most fascinating and rewarding journeys that anyone can take – the journey to a better realisation of self. The book is filled with easy-to-follow graphics, which show you at a simple glance how astrological patterns are working for you at any point in the year. Stage by stage, Old Moore's Astral Diaries will peel back the layers of your nature, allowing you a peek at the 'real you' in a way that is virtually impossible by any other means.

Old Moore extends his customary greeting to all people of the Earth and offers his age-old wishes for a happy and prosperous period ahead.

THE ESSENCE OF ARIES

Exploring the Personality of Aries the Ram

(21ST MARCH – 20TH APRIL)

What's in a sign?

Aries is not the first sign of the zodiac by accident. It's the place in the year when the spring begins, and so it represents some of the most dynamic forces in nature, and within the zodiac as a whole. As a result the very essence of your nature is geared towards promoting yourself in life and pushing your ideas forward very positively. You don't brook a great deal of interference in your life, but you are quite willing to help others as much as you can, provided that to do so doesn't curb your natural desire to get on in life.

Aries people are not universally liked, though your true friends remain loyal to you under almost any circumstances. But why should it be that such a dynamic and go-getting person does meet with some opposition? The answer is simple: not everyone is quite so sure of themselves as you are and many tend to get nervous when faced with the sheer power of the Aries personality. If there is one factor within your own control that could counter these problems it is the adoption of some humility – that commodity which is so important for you to dredge from the depths of your nature. If you only show the world that you are human, and that you are well aware of the fact, most people would follow you willingly to the very gates of hell. The most successful Aries subjects know this fact and cultivate it to the full.

Your executive skills are never in doubt and you can get almost anything practical done whilst others are still jumping from foot to foot. That's why you are such a good organiser and are so likely to be out there at the front of any venture. Adventurous and quite willing to show your bravery in public, you can even surprise yourself sometimes with the limits you are likely to go to in order to reach solutions that seem right to you.

Kind to those you take to, you can be universally loved when working at your best. Despite this there will be times in your life when you simply can't understand why some people just don't like you. Maybe there's an element of jealousy involved.

Aries resources

The part of the zodiac occupied by the sign of Aries has, for many centuries, been recognised as the home of self-awareness. This means that there isn't a person anywhere else in the zodiac that has a better knowledge of self than you do. But this isn't necessarily an intellectual process with Aries, more a response to the very blood that is coursing through your veins. Aries' success doesn't so much come from spending hours working out the pros and cons of any given course of action, more from the thrill of actually getting stuck in. If you find yourself forced into a life that means constantly having to think everything through to the tiniest detail, there is likely to be some frustration in evidence.

Aries is ruled by Mars, arguably the most go-getting of all the planets in the solar system. Mars is martial and demands practical ways of expressing latent power. It also requires absolute obedience from subordinates. When this is forthcoming, Aries individuals are the most magnanimous people to be found anywhere. Loyalty is not a problem and there have been many instances in history when Aries people were quite willing to die for their friends if necessary.

When other people are willing to give up and go with the flow, you will still be out there pitching for the result that seems most advantageous to you. It isn't something you can particularly control and those who don't know you well could find you sometimes curt and over-demanding as a result. But because you are tenacious you can pick the bones out of any situation and will usually arrive at your desired destination, if you don't collapse with fatigue on the way.

Routines, or having to take life at the pace of less motivated types, won't suit you at all. Imprisonment of any sort, even in a failed relationship, is sheer torture and you will move heaven and earth to get out into the big, wide world, where you can exploit your natural potential to the full. Few people know you really well because you don't always explain yourself adequately. The ones who do adore you.

Beneath the surface

Whereas some zodiac signs are likely to spend a great deal of their lives looking carefully at the innermost recesses of their own minds, Aries individuals tend to prefer the cut and thrust of the practical world. Aries people are not natural philosophers, but that doesn't mean that you aren't just as complicated beneath the surface as any of your astrological brothers and sisters. So what is it that makes the Aries firebrand think and act in the way that it does? To a great extent it is a lack of basic self-confidence.

This statement might seem rather odd, bearing in mind that a fair percentage of the people running our world were born under the sign of the Ram, but it is true nevertheless. Why? Because people who know themselves and their capabilities really well don't feel the constant need to prove themselves in the way that is the driving force of your zodiac sign. Not that your naturally progressive tendencies are a fault. On the contrary, if used correctly they can help you to create a much better, fairer and happier world, at least in your own vicinity.

The fact that you occasionally take your ball and go home if you can't get your own way is really down to the same insecurity that is noticeable through many facets of your nature. If Aries can't rule, it often doesn't want to play at all. A deep resentment and a brooding quality can build up in the minds and souls of some thwarted Aries types, a tendency that you need to combat. Better by far to try and compromise, itself a word that doesn't exist in the vocabularies of the least enlightened people born under the sign of the Ram. Once this lesson is learned, inner happiness increases and you relax into your life much more.

The way you think about others is directly related to the way you consider they think about you. This leads to another surprising fact regarding the zodiac sign. Aries people absolutely hate to be disliked, though they would move heaven and earth to prove that this isn't the case. And as a result Aries both loves and hates with a passion. Deep inside you can sometimes be a child shivering in the dark. If you only realise this fact your path to happiness and success is almost assured. Of course to do so takes a good deal of courage – but that's a commodity you don't lack.

Making the best of yourself

It would be quite clear to any observer that you are not the sort of person who likes to hang around at the back of a queue, or who would relish constantly taking orders from people who may not know situations as well as you do. For that reason alone you are better in positions that see you out there at the front, giving commands and enjoying the cut and thrust of everyday life. In a career sense this means that whatever you do you are happiest telling those around you how to do it too. Many Aries people quite naturally find their way to the top of the tree and don't usually have too much trouble staying there.

It is important to remember, however, that there is another side to your nature: the giving qualities beneath your natural dominance. You can always be around when people need you the most, encouraging and even gently pushing when it is necessary. By keeping friends and being willing to nurture relationships across a broad spectrum, you gradually get to know what makes those around you tick. This makes for a more patient and understanding sort of Aries subject – the most potent of all.

Even your resilience is not endless, which is why it is important to remember that there are times when you need rest. Bearing in mind that you are not superhuman is the hardest lesson to learn, but the admission brings humility, something that Aries needs to cultivate whenever possible.

Try to avoid living a restricted life and make your social contacts frequent and important. Realise that there is much more to life than work and spend some of your free time genuinely attempting to help those who are less well off than you are. Crucially you must remember that 'help' is not the same as domination.

The impressions you give

This section may well be of less interest to Aries subjects than it would be to certain other zodiac signs. The reason is quite clear. Aries people are far less interested in what others think about them than almost anyone else – or at least they tell themselves that they are. Either way it is counterproductive to ignore the opinions of the world at large because to do so creates stumbling blocks, even in a practical sense.

Those around you probably find you extremely capable and well able to deal with almost any situation that comes your way. Most are willing to rely heavily on you and the majority would almost instinctively see you as a leader. Whether or not they like you at the same time is really dependent on the way you handle situations. That's the difference between the go-getting, sometimes selfish type of Aries subject and the more enlightened amongst this illustrious sign.

You are viewed as being exciting and well able to raise enthusiasm for almost any project that takes your fancy. Of course this implies a great responsibility because you are always expected to come up with the goods. The world tends to put certain people on a pedestal, and you are one of them. On the other side of the coin we are all inclined to fire arrows at the elevated, so maintaining your position isn't very easy.

Most of the time you are seen as being magnanimous and kind, factors that you can exploit, whilst at the same time recognising the depth of the responsibility that comes with being an Aries subject. It might not be a bad thing to allow those around you to see that you too have feet of clay. This will make them respect and support you all the more, and even Aries people really do need to feel loved. A well-balanced Aries subject is one of the most elevated spirits to be found anywhere.

The way forward

You certainly enjoy life more when looking at it from the top of the tree. Struggling to get by is not in the least interesting to your zodiac sign and you can soon become miserable if things are not going well for you. That's why it is probably quite justified in your case to work tenaciously in order to achieve your objectives. Ideally, once you have realised some sort of success and security for yourself, you should then be willing to sit and watch life go by a little more. In fact this doesn't happen. The reason for this is clear. The Aries subject who learns how to succeed rarely knows when to stop – it's as simple as that.

Splitting your life into different components can help, if only because this means that you don't get the various elements mixed up. So, for example, don't confuse your love life with your professional needs, or your family with colleagues. This process allows you to view life in manageable chunks and also makes it possible for you to realise when any one of them may be working well. As a result you will put the effort where it's needed, and enjoy what is going well for you.

If you want to know real happiness you will also have to learn that acquisition for its own sake brings hollow rewards at best. When your talents are being turned outward to the world at large, you are one of the most potent and successful people around. What is more you should find yourself to be a much happier person when you are lending a hand to the wider world. This is possible, maybe outside of your normal professional sphere, though even where voluntary work is concerned it is important not to push yourself to the point of fatigue.

Keep yourself physically fit, without necessarily expecting that you can run to the South Pole and back, and stay away from too many stimulants, such as alcohol and nicotine. The fact is that you are best when living a healthy life, but it doesn't help either if you make even abstinence into an art form. Balance is important, as is moderation – itself a word that is difficult for you to understand. In terms of your approach to other people it's important to realise that everyone has a specific point of view. These might be different to yours, but they are not necessarily wrong. Sort out the friends who are most important to you and stick with them, whilst at the same time realising that almost everyone can be a pal – with just a little effort.

ARIES ON THE CUSP

Old Moore is often asked how astrological profiles are altered for those people born at either the beginning or the end of a zodiac sign, or, more properly, on the cusps of a sign. In the case of Aries this would be on the 21st of March and for two or three days after, and similarly at the end of the sign, probably from the 18th to the 20th of April. In this year's Astral Diaries, once again, Old Moore sets out to explain the differences regarding cuspid signs.

The Pisces Cusp – March 21st to March 24th

With the Sun so close to the zodiac sign of Pisces at the time you were born, it is distinctly possible that you have always had some doubts when reading a character breakdown written specifically for the sign of Aries. This isn't surprising because no zodiac sign has a definite start or end, they merely merge together. As a result there are some of the characteristics of the sign of the Fishes that are intermingled with the qualities of Aries in your nature.

What we probably find, as a result, is a greater degree of emotional sensitivity and a tendency to be more cognisant of what the rest of humanity is feeling. This is not to imply that Aries is unfeeling, but rather that Pisceans actively make humanity their business.

You are still able to achieve your most desired objectives in the practical world, but on the way, you stop to listen to the heartbeat of the planet on which you live. A very good thing, of course, but at the same time there is some conflict created if your slightly dream-like tendencies get in the way of your absolute need to see things through to their logical conclusion.

Nobody knows you better than you know yourself, or at least that's what the Aries qualities within you say, but that isn't always verified by some of the self-doubt that comes from the direction of the Fishes. As in all matters astrological, a position of balance has to be achieved in order to reconcile the differing qualities of your nature. In your case, this is best accomplished by being willing to stop and think once in a while and by refusing to allow your depth to be a problem.

Dealt with properly, the conjoining of Pisces and Aries can be a wondrous and joyful affair, a harmony of opposites that always makes you interesting to know. Your position in the world is naturally one of authority but at the same time you need to serve. That's why some people with this sort of mixture of astrological qualities would make such good administrators in a hospital, or in any position where the alternate astrological needs are well balanced. In the chocolate box of life you are certainly a 'soft centre'.

The Taurus Cusp – April 18th to April 20th

The merge from Aries to Taurus is much less well defined than the one at the other side of Aries, but it can be very useful to you all the same. Like the Pisces-influenced Aries you may be slightly more quiet than would be the case with the Ram taken alone and your thought processes are probably not quite as fast. But to compensate for this fact you don't rush into things quite as much and are willing to allow ideas to mature more fully.

Your sense of harmony and beauty is strong and you know, in a very definite way, exactly what you want. As a result your home will be distinctive but tasteful and it's a place where you need space to be alone sometimes, which the true Aries subject probably does not. You do not lack the confidence to make things look the way you want them, but you have a need to display these things to the world at large and sometimes even to talk about how good you are at decoration and design.

If anyone finds you pushy, it is probably because they don't really know what makes you tick. Although you are willing to mix with almost anyone, you are more inclined, at base, to have a few very close friends who stay at the forefront of your life for a long time. It is likely that you enjoy refined company and you wouldn't take kindly to the dark, the sordid, or the downright crude in life.

Things don't get you down as much as can sometimes be seen to be the case for Taurus when taken alone and you are rarely stumped for a progressive and practical idea when one is needed most. At all levels, your creative energy is evident and some of you even have the ability to make this into a business, since Aries offers the practical and administrative spark that Taurus can sometimes lack.

In matters of love, you are ardent and sincere, probably an idealist, and you know what you want in a partner. Whilst this is also true in the case of Taurus, you are different, because you are much more likely, not only to look, but also to say something about the way you feel.

Being naturally friendly you rarely go short of the right sort of help and support when it is most vital. Part of the reason for this lies in the fact that you are so willing to be the sounding-board for the concerns of your friends. All in all you can be very contented with your lot, but you never stop searching for something better all the same. At its best, this is one of the most progressive cuspal matches of them all.

ARIES AND ITS ASCENDANTS

The nature of every individual on the planet is composed of the rich variety of zodiac signs and planetary positions that were present at the time of their birth. Your Sun sign, which in your case is Aries, is one of the many factors when it comes to assessing the unique person you are. Probably the most important consideration, other than your Sun sign, is to establish the zodiac sign that was rising over the eastern horizon at the time that you were born. This is your Ascending or Rising sign. Most popular astrology fails to take account of the Ascendant, and yet its importance remains with you from the very moment of your birth, through every day of your life. The Ascendant is evident in the way you approach the world, and so, when meeting a person for the first time, it is this astrological influence that you are most likely to notice first. Our Ascending sign essentially represents what we appear to be, while our Sun sign is what we feel inside ourselves.

The Ascendant also has the potential for modifying our overall nature. For example, if you were born at a time of day when Aries was passing over the eastern horizon (this would be around the time of dawn) then you would be classed as a double Aries. As such you would typify this zodiac sign, both internally and in your dealings with others. However, if your Ascendant sign turned out to be a Water sign, such as Pisces, there would be a profound alteration of nature, away from the expected qualities of Aries.

One of the reasons that popular astrology often ignores the Ascendant is that it has always been rather difficult to establish. Old Moore has found a way to make this possible by devising an easy-to-use table, which you will find on page 157 of this book. Using this, you can establish your Ascendant sign at a glance. You will need to know your rough time of birth, then it is simply a case of following the instructions.

For those readers who have no idea of their time of birth it might be worth allowing a good friend, or perhaps your partner, to read through the section that follows this introduction. Someone who deals with you on a regular basis may easily discover your Ascending sign, even though you could have some difficulty establishing it for yourself. A good understanding of this component of your nature is essential if you want to be aware of that 'other person' who is responsible for the way you make contact with the world at large. Your Sun sign, Ascendant sign, and the other pointers in this book will, together, allow you a far better understanding of what makes you tick as an individual. Peeling back the different layers of your astrological make-up can be an enlightening experience, and the Ascendant may represent one of the most important layers of all.

Aries with Aries Ascendant

What you see is what you get with this combination. You typify the no-nonsense approach of Aries at its best. All the same this combination is quite daunting when viewed through the eyes of other, less dominant sorts of people. You tend to push your way though situations that would find others cowering in a corner and you are afraid of very little. With a determination to succeed that makes you a force to be reckoned with, you leave the world in no doubt as to your intentions and tend to be rather too brusque for your own good on occasions.

At heart you are kind and loving, able to offer assistance to the downtrodden and sad, and usually willing to take on board the cares of people who have a part to play in your life. No-one would doubt your sincerity, or your honesty, though you may utilise slightly less than orthodox ways of getting your own way on those occasions when you feel you have right on your side. You are a loving partner and a good parent, though where children are concerned you tend to be rather too protective. The trouble is that you know what a big, bad world it can be and probably feel that you are better equipped to deal with things than anyone else.

Aries with Taurus Ascendant

This is a much quieter combination, so much so that even experienced astrologers would be unlikely to recognise you as an Aries subject at all, unless of course they came to know you very well. Your approach to life tends to be quiet and considered and there is a great danger that you could suppress those feelings that others of your kind would be only too willing to verbalise. To compensate you are deeply creative and will think matters through much more readily than more dominant Aries types would be inclined to do. Reaching out towards the world, you are, nevertheless, somewhat locked inside yourself and can struggle to achieve the level of communication that you so desperately need. Frustration might easily follow, were it not for the fact that you possess a quiet determination that, to those in the know, is the clearest window through to your Aries soul.

The care for others is stronger here than with almost any other Aries type and you certainly demonstrate this at all levels. The fact is that you live a great percentage of your life in service to the people you take to, whilst at the same time being able to shut the door firmly in the face of people who irritate or anger you. You are deeply motivated towards family relationships.

Aries with Gemini Ascendant

A fairly jolly combination this, though by no means easy for others to come to terms with. You fly about from pillar to post and rarely stop long enough to take a breath. Admittedly this suits your own needs very well, but it can be a source of some disquiet to those around you, since they may not possess your energy or motivation. Those who know you well are deeply in awe of your capacity to keep going long after almost everyone else would have given up and gone home, though this quality is not always as wonderful as it sounds because it means that you put more pressure on your nervous system than just about any other astrological combination.

You need to be mindful of your nervous system, which responds to the erratic, mercurial quality of Gemini. Problems only really arise when the Aries part of you makes demands that the Gemini component finds difficult to deal with. There are paradoxes galore here and some of them need sorting out if you are ever fully to understand yourself, or are to be in a position when others know what makes you tick.

In relationships you might be a little fickle, but you are a real charmer and never stuck for the right words, no matter who you are dealing with. Your tenacity knows no bounds, though perhaps it should!

Aries with Cancer Ascendant

The main problem that you experience in life shows itself as a direct result of the meshing of these two very different zodiac signs. At heart Aries needs to dominate, whereas Cancer shows a desire to nurture. All too often the result can be a protective arm that is so strong that nobody could possibly get out from under it. Lighten your own load, and that of those you care for, by being willing to sit back and watch others please themselves a little. You might think that you know best, and your heart is clearly in the right place, but try to realise what life is like when someone is always on hand to tell you that they know better then you do.

But in a way this is a little severe, because you are fairly intuitive and your instincts would rarely lead you astray. Nobody could ask for a better partner or parent than you, though they might request a slightly less attentive one. In matters of work you are conscientious and are probably best suited to a job that means sorting out the kind of mess that humanity is so good at creating. You probably spend your spare time untangling balls of wool, though you are quite sporting too and could easily make the Olympics. Once there you would not win however, because you would be too concerned about all the other competitors.

Aries with Leo Ascendant

Here we come upon the first situation of Aries being allied with another Fire sign. This creates a character that could appear to be typically Aries at first sight and in many ways it is, though there are subtle differences that should not be ignored. Although you have the typical Aries ability to get things done, many of the tasks you do undertake will be for and on behalf of others. You can be proud, and on some occasions even haughty, and yet you are also regal in your bearing and honest to the point of absurdity. Nobody could doubt your sincerity and you have the soul of a poet combined with the courage of a lion.

All this is good, but it makes you rather difficult to approach, unless the person in question has first adopted a crouching and subservient attitude although you would not wish them to do so. It's simply that the impression you give and the motivation that underpins it are two quite different things. You are greatly respected and in the case of those individuals who know your real nature, you are also deeply loved. But life would be much simpler if you didn't always have to fight the wars that those around you are happy to start. Relaxation is a word that you don't really understand and you would do yourself a favour if you looked it up in a dictionary.

Aries with Virgo Ascendant

Virgo is steady and sure, though also fussy and stubborn. Aries is fast and determined, restless and active. It can already be seen that this is a rather strange meeting of characteristics and because Virgo is ruled by the capricious Mercury, the ultimate result will change from hour to hour and day to day. It isn't merely that others find it difficult to know where they are with you, they can't even understand what makes you tick. This will make you the subject of endless fascination and attention, at which you will be apparently surprised but inwardly pleased. If anyone ever really gets to know what goes on in that busy mind they may find the implications very difficult to deal with and it is a fact that only you would have the ability to live inside your crowded head.

As a partner and a parent you are second to none, though you tend to get on better with your children once they start to grow, since by this time you may be slightly less restricting to their own desires, which will often clash with your own on their behalf. You are capable of give and take and could certainly not be considered selfish, though your constant desire to get the best from everyone might occasionally be misconstrued.

Aries with Libra Ascendant

Libra has the tendency to bring out the best in any zodiac sign, and this is no exception when it comes together with Aries. You may, in fact, be the most comfortable of all Aries types, simply because Libra tempers some of your more assertive qualities and gives you the chance to balance out opposing forces, both inside yourself and in the world outside. You are fun to be with and make the staunchest friend possible. Although you are generally affable, few people would try to put one over on you, because they would quickly come to know how far you are willing to go before you let forth a string of invective that would shock those who previously underestimated your basic Aries traits.

Home and family are very dear to you, but you are more tolerant than some Aries types are inclined to be and you have a youthful zest for life that should stay with you no matter what age you manage to achieve. There is always something interesting to do and your mind is a constant stream of possibilities. This makes you very creative and you may also demonstrate a desire to look good at all times. You may not always be quite as confident as you appear to be, but few would guess the fact.

Aries with Scorpio Ascendant

The two very different faces of Mars come together in this potent, magnetic and quite awe-inspiring combination. Your natural inclination is towards secrecy and this fact, together with the natural attractions of the sensual Scorpio nature, makes you the object of great curiosity. This means that you will not go short of attention and should ensure that you are always being analysed by people who may never get to know you at all. At heart you prefer your own company, and yet life appears to find means to push you into the public gaze time and again. Most people with this combination ooze sex appeal and can use this fact as a stepping stone to personal success, yet without losing any integrity or loosening the cords of a deeply moralistic nature.

On those occasions when you do lose your temper, there isn't a character in the length and breadth of the zodiac who would have either the words or the courage to stand against the stream of invective that follows. On really rare occasions you might even scare yourself. As far as family members are concerned a simple look should be enough to show when you are not amused. Few people are left unmoved by your presence in their life.

Aries with Sagittarius Ascendant

What a lovely combination this can be, for the devil-may-care aspects of Sagittarius lighten the load of a sometimes too-serious Aries interior. Everything that glistens is not gold, though it's hard to convince you of the fact because, to mix metaphors, you can make a silk purse out of a sow's ear. Almost everyone loves you and in return you offer a friendship that is warm and protective, but not as demanding as sometimes tends to be the case with the Aries type. Relationships may be many and varied and there is often more than one major attachment in the life of those holding this combination. You will bring a breath of spring to any attachment, though you need to ensure that the person concerned is capable of keeping up with the hectic pace of your life

It may appear from time to time that you are rather too trusting for your own good, though deep inside you are very astute and it seems that almost everything you undertake works out well in the end. This has nothing to do with native luck and is really down to the fact that you are much more calculating than might appear to be the case at first sight. As a parent you are protective yet offer sufficient room for self-expression.

Aries with Capricorn Ascendant

If ever anyone could be accused of setting off immediately, but slowly, it has to be you. These are very contradictory signs and the differences will express themselves in a variety of ways. One thing is certain, you have tremendous tenacity and will see a job through patiently from beginning to end, without tiring on the way, and ensuring that every detail is taken care of properly. This combination often bestows good health and a great capacity for continuity, particularly in terms of the length of life. You are certainly not as argumentative as the typical Aries, but you do know how to get your own way, which is just as well because you are usually thinking on behalf of everyone else and not just on your own account.

At home you can relax, which is a blessing for Aries, though in fact you seldom choose to do so because you always have some project or other on the go. You probably enjoy knocking down and rebuilding walls, though this is a practical tendency and not responsive to relationships, in which you are ardent and sincere. Impetuosity is as close to your heart as is the case for any type of Aries subject, though you certainly have the ability to appear patient and steady. But it's just a front, isn't it?

Aries with Aquarius Ascendant

The person standing on a soap box in the corner of the park, extolling the virtues of this or that, could quite easily be an Aries with an Aquarian Ascendant. You are certainly not averse to speaking your mind and you have plenty to talk about because you are the best social reformer and political animal of them all. Unorthodox in your approach, you have the ability to keep everyone guessing, except when it comes to getting your own way, for in this nobody doubts your natural abilities. You can put theories into practice very well and on the way you retain a sense of individuality that would shock more conservative types. It's true that a few people might find you a little difficult to approach and this is partly because you have an inner reserve and strength which is difficult for others to fathom.

In the world at large you take your place at the front, as any good Arian should, and yet you offer room for others to share your platform. You keep up with the latest innovations and treat family members as the genuine friends that you believe them to be. Care needs to be taken when picking a life partner, for you are an original, and not just anyone could match the peculiarities thrown up by this astrological combination.

Aries with Pisces Ascendant

Although not an easy combination to deal with, the Aries with a Piscean Ascendant does, nevertheless, bring something very special to the world in the way of natural understanding allied to practical assistance. It's true that you can sometimes be a dreamer, but there is nothing wrong with that as long as you have the ability to turn some of your wishes into reality, and this you are easily able to do, usually for the sake of those around you. Conversation comes easily to you, though you also possess a slightly wistful and poetic side to your nature, which is attractive to the many people who call you a friend. A natural entertainer, you bring a sense of the comic to the often serious qualities of Aries, though without losing the determination that typifies the sign.

In relationships you are ardent, sincere and supportive, with a strong social conscience that sometimes finds you fighting the battles of the less privileged members of society. Family is important to you and this is a combination that invariably leads to parenthood. Away from the cut and thrust of everyday life you relax more fully and think about matters more deeply than more typical Aries types might.

THE MOON AND THE PART IT PLAYS IN YOUR LIFE

In astrology the Moon is probably the single most important heavenly body after the Sun. Its unique position, as partner to the Earth on its journey around the solar system, means that the Moon appears to pass through the signs of the zodiac extremely quickly. The zodiac position of the Moon at the time of your birth plays a great part in personal character and is especially significant in the build-up of your emotional nature.

Sun Moon Cycles

The first lunar cycle deals with the part the position of the Moon plays relative to your Sun sign. I have made the fluctuations of this pattern easy for you to understand by means of a simple cyclic graph. It appears on the first page of each 'Your Month At A Glance', under the title 'Highs and Lows'. The graph displays the lunar cycle and you will soon learn to understand how its movements have a bearing on your level of energy and your abilities.

Your Own Moon Sign

Discovering the position of the Moon at the time of your birth has always been notoriously difficult because tracking the complex zodiac positions of the Moon is not easy. This process has been reduced to three simple stages with Old Moore's unique Lunar Tables. A breakdown of the Moon's zodiac positions can be found from page 23 onwards, so that once you know what your Moon Sign is, you can see what part this plays in the overall build-up of your personal character.

If you follow the instructions on the next page you will soon be able to work out exactly what zodiac sign the Moon occupied on the day that you were born and you can then go on to compare the reading for this position with those of your Sun sign and your Ascendant. It is partly the comparison between these three important positions that goes towards making you the unique individual you are.

HOW TO DISCOVER YOUR MOON SIGN

This is a three-stage process. You may need a pen and a piece of paper but if you follow the instructions below the process should only take a minute or so.

STAGE 1 First of all you need to know the Moon Age at the time of your birth. If you look at Moon Table 1, on page 21, you will find all the years between 1907 and 2005 down the left side. Find the year of your birth and then trace across to the right to the month of your birth. Where the two intersect you will find a number. This is the date of the New Moon in the month that you were born. You now need to count forward the number of days between the New Moon and your own birthday. For example, if the New Moon in the month of your birth was shown as being the 6th and you were born on the 20th, your Moon Age Day would be 14. If the New Moon in the month of your birth came after your birthday, you need to count forward from the New Moon in the previous month. If you were born in a Leap Year, remember to count the 29th February. You can tell if your birth year was a Leap Year if the last two digits can be divided by four. Whatever the result, jot this number down so that you do not forget it.

STAGE 2 Take a look at Moon Table 2 on page 22. Down the left hand column look for the date of your birth. Now trace across to the month of your birth. Where the two meet you will find a letter. Copy this letter down alongside your Moon Age Day.

STAGE 3 Moon Table 3 on page 22 will supply you with the zodiac sign the Moon occupied on the day of your birth. Look for your Moon Age Day down the left hand column and then for the letter you found in Stage 2. Where the two converge you will find a zodiac sign and this is the sign occupied by the Moon on the day that you were born.

Your Zodiac Moon Sign Explained

You will find a profile of all zodiac Moon Signs on pages 23 to 26, showing in yet another way how astrology helps to make you into the individual that you are. In each daily entry of the Astral Diary you can find the zodiac position of the Moon for every day of the year. This also allows you to discover your lunar birthdays. Since the Moon passes through all the signs of the zodiac in about a month, you can expect something like twelve lunar birthdays each year. At these times you are likely to be emotionally steady and able to make the sort of decisions that have real, lasting value.

MOON TABLE 1

YEAR	FEB	MAR	APR	YEAR	FEB	MAR	APR	YEAR	FEB	MAR	APR
1907	12	14	12	1940	8	9	7	1973	4	5	3
1908	2	3	2	1941	26	27	26	1974	22	24	22
1909	20	21	20	1942	15	16	15	1975	11	12	11
1910	9	11	9	1943	4	6	4	1976	29	30	29
1911	28	30	28	1944	24	24	22	1977	18	19	18
1912	17	19	18	1945	12	14	12	1978	7	9	7
1913	6	7	6	1946	2	3	2	1979	26	27	26
1914	24	26	24	1947	19	21	20	1980	15	16	15
1915	14	15	13	1948	9	11	9	1981	4	6	4
1916	3	5	3	1949	27	29	28	1982	23	24	23
1917	22	23	22	1950	16	18	17	1983	13	14	13
1918	11	12	11	1951	6	7	6	1984	1	2	1
1919	–	2/31	30	1952	25	25	24	1985	19	21	20
1920	19	20	18	1953	14	15	13	1986	9	10	9
1921	8	9	8	1954	3	5	3	1987	28	29	28
1922	26	28	27	1955	22	24	22	1988	17	18	16
1923	15	17	16	1956	11	12	11	1989	6	7	6
1924	5	5	4	1957	–	1/31	29	1990	25	26	25
1925	23	24	23	1958	18	20	19	1991	14	15	13
1926	12	14	12	1959	7	9	8	1992	3	4	3
1927	2	3	2	1960	26	27	26	1993	22	24	22
1928	19	21	20	1961	15	16	15	1994	10	12	11
1929	9	11	9	1962	5	6	5	1995	29	30	29
1930	28	30	28	1963	23	25	23	1996	18	19	18
1931	17	19	18	1964	13	14	12	1997	7	9	7
1932	6	7	6	1965	1	2	1	1998	26	27	26
1933	24	26	24	1966	19	21	20	1999	16	17	16
1934	14	15	13	1967	9	10	9	2000	5	6	4
1935	3	5	3	1968	28	29	28	2001	23	24	23
1936	22	23	21	1969	17	18	16	2002	12	13	12
1937	11	13	12	1970	6	7	6	2003	–	2	1
1938	–	2/31	30	1971	25	26	25	2004	20	21	19
1939	19	20	19	1972	14	15	13	2005	9	10	8

TABLE 2

MOON TABLE 3

DAY	MAR	APR
1	F	J
2	G	J
3	G	J
4	G	J
5	G	J
6	G	J
7	G	J
8	G	J
9	G	J
10	G	J
11	G	K
12	H	K
13	H	K
14	H	K
15	H	K
16	H	K
17	H	K
18	H	K
19	H	K
20	H	K
21	H	L
22	I	L
23	I	L
24	I	L
25	I	L
26	I	L
27	I	L
28	I	L
29	I	L
30	I	L
31	I	–

M/D	F	G	H	I	J	K	L
0	PI	PI	AR	AR	AR	TA	TA
1	PI	AR	AR	AR	TA	TA	TA
2	AR	AR	AR	TA	TA	TA	GE
3	AR	AR	TA	TA	TA	GE	GE
4	AR	TA	TA	GE	GE	GE	GE
5	TA	TA	GE	GE	GE	CA	CA
6	TA	GE	GE	GE	CA	CA	CA
7	GE	GE	GE	CA	CA	CA	LE
8	GE	GE	CA	CA	CA	LE	LE
9	CA	CA	CA	CA	LE	LE	VI
10	CA	CA	LE	LE	LE	VI	VI
11	CA	LE	LE	LE	VI	VI	VI
12	LE	LE	LE	VI	VI	VI	LI
13	LE	LE	VI	VI	VI	LI	LI
14	VI	VI	VI	LI	LI	LI	LI
15	VI	VI	LI	LI	LI	SC	SC
16	VI	LI	LI	LI	SC	SC	SC
17	LI	LI	LI	SC	SC	SC	SA
18	LI	LI	SC	SC	SC	SA	SA
19	LI	SC	SC	SC	SA	SA	SA
20	SC	SC	SA	SA	SA	CP	CP
21	SC	SA	SA	SA	CP	CP	CP
22	SC	SA	SA	CP	CP	CP	AQ
23	SA	SA	CP	CP	CP	AQ	AQ
24	SA	CP	CP	CP	AQ	AQ	AQ
25	CP	CP	AQ	AQ	AQ	PI	PI
26	CP	AQ	AQ	AQ	PI	PI	PI
27	AQ	AQ	AQ	PI	PI	PI	AR
28	AQ	AQ	PI	PI	PI	AR	AR
29	AQ	PI	PI	PI	AR	AR	AR

AR = Aries, TA = Taurus, GE = Gemini, CA = Cancer, LE = Leo, VI = Virgo, LI = Libra, SC = Scorpio, SA = Sagittarius, CP = Capricorn, AQ = Aquarius, PI = Pisces

MOON SIGNS

Moon in Aries

You have a strong imagination, courage, determination and a desire to do things in your own way and forge your own path through life.

Originality is a key attribute; you are seldom stuck for ideas although your mind is changeable and you could take the time to focus on individual tasks. Often quick-tempered, you take orders from few people and live life at a fast pace. Avoid health problems by taking regular time out for rest and relaxation.

Emotionally, it is important that you talk to those you are closest to and work out your true feelings. Once you discover that people are there to help, there is less necessity for you to do everything yourself.

Moon in Taurus

The Moon in Taurus gives you a courteous and friendly manner, which means you are likely to have many friends.

The good things in life mean a lot to you, as Taurus is an Earth sign that delights in experiences which please the senses. Hence you are probably a lover of good food and drink, which may in turn mean you need to keep an eye on the bathroom scales, especially as looking good is also important to you.

Emotionally you are fairly stable and you stick by your own standards. Taureans do not respond well to change. Intuition also plays an important part in your life.

Moon in Gemini

You have a warm-hearted character, sympathetic and eager to help others. At times reserved, you can also be articulate and chatty: this is part of the paradox of Gemini, which always brings duplicity to the nature. You are interested in current affairs, have a good intellect, and are good company and likely to have many friends. Most of your friends have a high opinion of you and would be ready to defend you should the need arise. However, this is usually unnecessary, as you are quite capable of defending yourself in any verbal confrontation.

Travel is important to your inquisitive mind and you find intellectual stimulus in mixing with people from different cultures. You also gain much from reading, writing and the arts but you do need plenty of rest and relaxation in order to avoid fatigue.

Moon in Cancer

The Moon in Cancer at the time of birth is a fortunate position as Cancer is the Moon's natural home. This means that the qualities of compassion and understanding given by the Moon are especially enhanced in your nature, and you are friendly and sociable and cope well with emotional pressures. You cherish home and family life, and happily do the domestic tasks. Your surroundings are important to you and you hate squalor and filth. You are likely to have a love of music and poetry.

Your basic character, although at times changeable like the Moon itself, depends on symmetry. You aim to make your surroundings comfortable and harmonious, for yourself and those close to you.

Moon in Leo

The best qualities of the Moon and Leo come together to make you warm-hearted, fair, ambitious and self-confident. With good organisational abilities, you invariably rise to a position of responsibility in your chosen career. This is fortunate as you don't enjoy being an 'also-ran' and would rather be an important part of a small organisation than a menial in a large one.

You should be lucky in love, and happy, provided you put in the effort to make a comfortable home for yourself and those close to you. It is likely that you will have a love of pleasure, sport, music and literature. Life brings you many rewards, most of them as a direct result of your own efforts, although you may be luckier than average and ready to make the best of any situation.

Moon in Virgo

You are endowed with good mental abilities and a keen receptive memory, but you are never ostentatious or pretentious. Naturally quite reserved, you still have many friends, especially of the opposite sex. Marital relationships must be discussed carefully and worked at so that they remain harmonious, as personal attachments can be a problem if you do not give them your full attention.

Talented and persevering, you possess artistic qualities and are a good homemaker. Earning your honours through genuine merit, you work long and hard towards your objectives but show little pride in your achievements. Many short journeys will be undertaken in your life.

Moon in Libra

With the Moon in Libra you are naturally popular and make friends easily. People like you, probably more than you realise, you bring fun to a party and are a natural diplomat. For all its good points, Libra is not the most stable of astrological signs and, as a result, your emotions can be a little unstable too. Therefore, although the Moon in Libra is said to be good for love and marriage, your Sun sign and Rising sign will have an important effect on your emotional and loving qualities.

You must remember to relate to others in your decision-making. Co-operation is crucial because Libra represents the 'balance' of life that can only be achieved through harmonious relationships. Conformity is not easy for you because Libra, an Air sign, likes its independence.

Moon in Scorpio

Some people might call you pushy. In fact, all you really want to do is to live life to the full and protect yourself and your family from the pressures of life. Take care to avoid giving the impression of being sarcastic or impulsive and use your energies wisely and constructively.

You have great courage and you invariably achieve your goals by force of personality and sheer effort. You are fond of mystery and are good at predicting the outcome of situations and events. Travel experiences can be beneficial to you.

You may experience problems if you do not take time to examine your motives in a relationship, and also if you allow jealousy, always a feature of Scorpio, to cloud your judgement.

Moon in Sagittarius

The Moon in Sagittarius helps to make you a generous individual with humanitarian qualities and a kind heart. Restlessness may be intrinsic as your mind is seldom still. Perhaps because of this, you have a need for change that could lead you to several major moves during your adult life. You are not afraid to stand your ground when you know your judgement is right, you speak directly and have good intuition.

At work you are quick, efficient and versatile and so you make an ideal employee. You need work to be intellectually demanding and do not enjoy tedious routines.

In relationships, you anger quickly if faced with stupidity or deception, though you are just as quick to forgive and forget. Emotionally, there are times when your heart rules your head.

Moon in Capricorn

The Moon in Capricorn makes you popular and likely to come into the public eye in some way. The watery Moon is not entirely comfortable in the Earth sign of Capricorn and this may lead to some difficulties in the early years of life. An initial lack of creative ability and indecision must be overcome before the true qualities of patience and perseverance inherent in Capricorn can show through.

You have good administrative ability and are a capable worker, and if you are careful you can accumulate wealth. But you must be cautious and take professional advice in partnerships, as you are open to deception. You may be interested in social or welfare work, which suit your organisational skills and sympathy for others.

Moon in Aquarius

The Moon in Aquarius makes you an active and agreeable person with a friendly, easy-going nature. Sympathetic to the needs of others, you flourish in a laid-back atmosphere. You are broad-minded, fair and open to suggestion, although sometimes you have an unconventional quality which others can find hard to understand.

You are interested in the strange and curious, and in old articles and places. You enjoy trips to these places and gain much from them. Political, scientific and educational work interests you and you might choose a career in science or technology.

Money-wise, you make gains through innovation and concentration and Lunar Aquarians often tackle more than one job at a time. In love you are kind and honest.

Moon in Pisces

You have a kind, sympathetic nature, somewhat retiring at times, but you always take account of others' feelings and help when you can.

Personal relationships may be problematic, but as life goes on you can learn from your experiences and develop a better understanding of yourself and the world around you.

You have a fondness for travel, appreciate beauty and harmony and hate disorder and strife. You may be fond of literature and would make a good writer or speaker yourself. You have a creative imagination and may come across as an incurable romantic. You have strong intuition, maybe bordering on a mediumistic quality, which sets you apart from the mass. You may not be rich in cash terms, but your personal gifts are worth more than gold.

ARIES IN LOVE

Discover how compatible in love you are with people from the same and other signs of the zodiac. Five stars equals a match made in heaven!

Aries meets Aries

This could be be an all-or-nothing pairing. Both parties are from a dominant sign, so someone will have to be flexible in order to maintain personal harmony. Both know what they want out of life, and may have trouble overcoming any obstacles a relationship creates. This is a good physical pairing, with a chemistry that few other matches enjoy to the same level. Attitude is everything, but at least there is a mutual admiration that makes gazing at your partner like looking in the mirror. Star rating: ****

Aries meets Taurus

This is a match that has been known to work very well. Aries brings dynamism and ambition, while Taurus has the patience to see things through logically. Such complementary views work equally well in a relationship or in the office. There is mutual respect, but sometimes a lack of total understanding. The romantic needs of each are quite different, but both are still fulfilled. They can live easily in domestic harmony which is very important but, interestingly, Aries may be the loser in battles of will. Star rating: ***

Aries meets Gemini

Don't expect peace and harmony with this combination, although what comes along instead might make up for any disagreements. Gemini has a very fertile imagination, while Aries has the tenacity to make reality from fantasy. Combined, they have a sizzling relationship. There are times when both parties could explode with indignation and something has to give. But even if there are clashes, making them up will always be most enjoyable! Mutual financial success is likely in this match. Star rating: ****

Aries meets Cancer

A potentially one-sided pairing, it often appears that the Cancerian is brow-beaten by the far more dominant Arian. So much depends on the patience of the Cancerian individual, because if good psychology is present – who knows? But beware, Aries, you may find your partner too passive, and constantly having to take the lead can be wearing – even for you. A prolonged trial period would be advantageous, as the match could easily go either way. When it does work, though, this relationship is usually contented. Star rating: ***

Aries meets Leo

Stand by for action and make sure the house is sound-proof. Leo is a lofty idealist and there is always likely to be friction when two Fire signs meet. To compensate, there is much mutual admiration, together with a desire to please. Where there are shared incentives, the prognosis is good but it's important not to let little irritations blow up. Both signs want to have their own way and this is a sure cause of trouble. There might not be much patience here, but there is plenty of action. Star rating: *****

Aries meets Virgo

Neither of these signs really understands the other, and that could easily lead to a clash. Virgo is so pedantic, which will drive Aries up the wall, while Aries always wants to be moving on to the next objective, before Virgo is even settled with the last one. It will take time for these two to get to know each other, but this is a great business matching. If a personal relationship is seen in these terms then the prognosis can be good, but on the whole, this is not an inspiring match. Star rating: ***

Aries meets Libra

These signs are zodiac opposites which means a make-or-break situation. The match will either be a great success or a dismal failure. Why? Well Aries finds it difficult to understand the flighty Air-sign tendencies of Libra, whilst the natural balance of Libra contradicts the unorthodox Arian methods. Any flexibility will come from Libra, which may mean that things work out for a while, but Libra only has so much patience and it may eventually run out. In the end, Aries may be just too bossy for an independent but sensitive sign like Libra. Star rating: **

Aries meets Scorpio

There can be great affection here, even if the two zodiac signs are so very different. The common link is the planet Mars, which plays a part in both these natures. Although Aries is, outwardly, the most dominant, Scorpio people are among the most powerful to be found anywhere. This quiet determination is respected by Aries. Aries will satisfy the passionate side of Scorpio, particularly with instruction from Scorpio. There are mysteries here which will add spice to life. The few arguments that do occur are likely to be awe-inspiring. Star rating: ****

Aries meets Sagittarius

This can be one of the most favourable matches of them all. Both Aries and Sagittarius are Fire signs, which often leads to clashes of will, but this pair find a mutual understanding. Sagittarius helps Aries to develop a better sense of humour, while Aries teaches the Archer about consistency on the road to success. Some patience is called for on both sides, but these people have a natural liking for each other. Add this to growing love and you have a long-lasting combination that is hard to beat. Star rating: *****

Aries meets Capricorn

Capricorn works conscientiously to achieve its objectives and so can be the perfect companion for Aries. The Ram knows how to achieve but not how to consolidate, so the two signs have a great deal to offer one another practically. There may not be fireworks and it's sometimes doubtful how well they know each other, but it may not matter. Aries is outwardly hot but inwardly cool, whilst Capricorn can appear low key but be a furnace underneath. Such a pairing can gradually find contentment, though both parties may wonder how this is so. Star rating: ****

Aries meets Aquarius

Aquarius is an Air sign, and Air and Fire often work well together, but perhaps not in the case of Aries and Aquarius. The average Aquarian lives in what the Ram sees as a fantasy world, so without a sufficiently good meeting of minds, compromise may be lacking. Of course, almost anything is possible, and the dominant side of Aries could be trained by the devil-may-care attitude of Aquarius. There are meeting points but they are difficult to establish. However, given sufficient time and an open mind on both sides, a degree of happiness is possible. Star rating: **

Aries meets Pisces

Still waters run deep, and they don't come much deeper than Pisces. Although these signs share the same quadrant of the zodiac, they have little in common. Pisces is a dreamer, a romantic idealist with steady and spiritual goals. Aries needs to be on the move, and has very different ideals. It's hard to see how a relationship could develop because the outlook on life is so different but, with patience, especially from Aries, there is a chance that things might work out. Pisces needs incentive, and Aries may be the sign to offer it. Star rating: **

VENUS:
THE PLANET OF LOVE

If you look up at the sky around sunset or sunrise you will often see Venus in close attendance to the Sun. It is arguably one of the most beautiful sights of all and there is little wonder that historically it became associated with the goddess of love. But although Venus does play an important part in the way you view love and in the way others see you romantically, this is only one of the spheres of influence that it enjoys in your overall character.

Venus has a part to play in the more cultured side of your life and has much to do with your appreciation of art, literature, music and general creativity. Even the way you look is responsive to the part of the zodiac that Venus occupied at the start of your life, though this fact is also down to your Sun sign and Ascending sign. If, at the time you were born, Venus occupied one of the more gregarious zodiac signs, you will be more likely to wear your heart on your sleeve, as well as to be more attracted to entertainment, social gatherings and good company. If on the other hand Venus occupied a quiet zodiac sign at the time of your birth, you would tend to be more retiring and less willing to shine in public situations.

It's good to know what part the planet Venus plays in your life for it can have a great bearing on the way you appear to the rest of the world and since we all have to mix with others, you can learn to make the very best of what Venus has to offer you.

One of the great complications in the past has always been trying to establish exactly what zodiac position Venus enjoyed when you were born because the planet is notoriously difficult to track. However, I have solved that problem by creating a table that is exclusive to your Sun sign, which you will find on the following page.

Establishing your Venus sign could not be easier. Just look up the year of your birth on the page opposite and you will see a sign of the zodiac. This was the sign that Venus occupied in the period covered by your sign in that year. If Venus occupied more than one sign during the period, this is indicated by the date on which the sign changed, and the name of the new sign. For instance, if you were born in 1950, Venus was in Aquarius until the 7th April, after which time it was in Pisces. If you were born before 7th April your Venus sign is Aquarius, if you were born on or after 7th April, your Venus sign is Pisces. Once you have established the position of Venus at the time of your birth, you can then look in the pages which follow to see how this has a bearing on your life as a whole.

1907 AQUARIUS / 2.4 PISCES
1908 TAURUS / 8.4 GEMINI
1909 PISCES / 29.3 ARIES
1910 AQUARIUS / 5.4 PISCES
1911 ARIES / 25.3 TAURUS
1912 PISCES / 14.4 ARIES
1913 TAURUS
1914 ARIES /14.4 TAURUS
1915 AQUARIUS / 1.4 PISCES
1916 TAURUS / 8.4 GEMINI
1917 PISCES / 28.3 ARIES
1918 AQUARIUS / 5.4 PISCES
1919 ARIES / 24.3 TAURUS
1920 PISCES / 14.4 ARIES
1921 TAURUS
1922 ARIES / 13.4 TAURUS
1923 AQUARIUS / 1.4 PISCES
1924 TAURUS / 6.4 GEMINI
1925 PISCES / 28.3 ARIES
1926 AQUARIUS / 6.4 PISCES
1927 ARIES / 24.3 TAURUS
1928 PISCES / 13.4 ARIES
1929 TAURUS / 20.4 ARIES
1930 ARIES / 13.4 TAURUS
1931 AQUARIUS / 31.3 PISCES
1932 TAURUS / 6.4 GEMINI
1933 PISCES / 27.3 ARIES
1934 AQUARIUS / 6.4 PISCES
1935 ARIES / 23.3 TAURUS
1936 PISCES / 13.4 ARIES
1937 TAURUS / 14.4 ARIES
1938 ARIES / 12.4 TAURUS
1939 AQUARIUS / 31.3 PISCES
1940 TAURUS / 5.4 GEMINI
1941 PISCES / 26.3 ARIES /
     20.4 TAURUS
1942 AQUARIUS / 7.4 PISCES
1943 ARIES / 23.3 TAURUS
1944 PISCES / 12.4 ARIES
1945 TAURUS / 8.4 ARIES
1946 ARIES / 12.4 TAURUS
1947 AQUARIUS / 30.3 PISCES
1948 TAURUS / 5.4 GEMINI
1949 PISCES / 25.3 ARIES /
     20.4 TAURUS
1950 AQUARIUS / 7.4 PISCES
1951 ARIES / 22.3 TAURUS
1952 PISCES / 12.4 ARIES
1953 TAURUS / 1.4 ARIES
1954 ARIES / 11.4 TAURUS
1955 AQUARIUS / 30.3 PISCES
1956 TAURUS / 4.4 GEMINI
1957 PISCES / 25.3 ARIES /
     19.4 TAURUS

1958 AQUARIUS / 8.4 PISCES
1959 ARIES / 22.3 TAURUS
1960 PISCES / 11.4 ARIES
1961 ARIES
1962 ARIES / 11.4 TAURUS
1963 AQUARIUS / 29.3 PISCES
1964 TAURUS / 4.4 GEMINI
1965 PISCES / 24.3 ARIES /
     19.4 TAURUS
1966 AQUARIUS / 8.4 PISCES
1967 TAURUS / 20.4 GEMINI
1968 PISCES / 10.4 ARIES
1969 ARIES
1970 ARIES / 10.4 TAURUS
1971 AQUARIUS / 29.3 PISCES
1972 TAURUS / 3.4 GEMINI
1973 PISCES / 24.3 ARIES /
     18.4 TAURUS
1974 AQUARIUS / 8.4 PISCES
1975 TAURUS / 19.4 GEMINI
1976 PISCES / 10.4 ARIES
1977 ARIES
1978 ARIES / 10.4 TAURUS
1979 AQUARIUS / 28.3 PISCES
1980 TAURUS / 3.4 GEMINI
1981 PISCES / 23.3 ARIES /
     18.4 TAURUS
1982 AQUARIUS / 9.4 PISCES
1983 TAURUS / 19.4 GEMINI
1984 PISCES / 9.4 ARIES
1985 ARIES
1986 ARIES / 9.4 TAURUS
1987 AQUARIUS / 28.3 PISCES
1988 TAURUS / 2.4 GEMINI
1989 PISCES / 23.3 ARIES /
     17.4 TAURUS
1990 AQUARIUS / 9.4 PISCES
1991 TAURUS / 18.4 GEMINI
1992 PISCES / 9.4 ARIES
1993 ARIES
1994 ARIES / 9.4 TAURUS
1995 AQUARIUS / 27.3 PISCES
1996 TAURUS / 2.4 GEMINI
1997 PISCES / 22.3 ARIES /
     17.4 TAURUS
1998 AQUARIUS / 9.4 PISCES
1999 TAURUS / 18.4 GEMINI
2000 PISCES / 9.4 ARIES
2001 ARIES
2002 ARIES / 7.4 TAURUS
2003 AQUARIUS / 27.3 PISCES
2004 TAURUS / 1.4 GEMINI
2005 PISCES/22.3 ARIES

VENUS THROUGH THE ZODIAC SIGNS

Venus in Aries

Amongst other things, the position of Venus in Aries indicates a fondness for travel, music and all creative pursuits. Your nature tends to be affectionate and you would try not to create confusion or difficulty for others if it could be avoided. Many people with this planetary position have a great love of the theatre, and mental stimulation is of the greatest importance. Early romantic attachments are common with Venus in Aries, so it is very important to establish a genuine sense of romantic continuity. Early marriage is not recommended, especially if it is based on sympathy. You may give your heart a little too readily on occasions.

Venus in Taurus

You are capable of very deep feelings and your emotions tend to last for a very long time. This makes you a trusting partner and lover, whose constancy is second to none. In life you are precise and careful and always try to do things the right way. Although this means an ordered life, which you are comfortable with, it can also lead you to be rather too fussy for your own good. Despite your pleasant nature, you are very fixed in your opinions and quite able to speak your mind. Others are attracted to you and historical astrologers always quoted this position of Venus as being very fortunate in terms of marriage. However, if you find yourself involved in a failed relationship, it could take you a long time to trust again.

Venus in Gemini

As with all associations related to Gemini, you tend to be quite versatile, anxious for change and intelligent in your dealings with the world at large. You may gain money from more than one source but you are equally good at spending it. There is an inference here that you are a good communicator, via either the written or the spoken word, and you love to be in the company of interesting people. Always on the look-out for culture, you may also be very fond of music, and love to indulge the curious and cultured side of your nature. In romance you tend to have more than one relationship and could find yourself associated with someone who has previously been a friend or even a distant relative.

Venus in Cancer

You often stay close to home because you are very fond of family and enjoy many of your most treasured moments when you are with those you love. Being naturally sympathetic, you will always do anything you can to support those around you, even people you hardly know at all. This charitable side of your nature is your most noticeable trait and is one of the reasons why others are naturally so fond of you. Being receptive and in some cases even psychic, you can see through to the soul of most of those with whom you come into contact. You may not commence too many romantic attachments but when you do give your heart, it tends to be unconditionally.

Venus in Leo

It must become quickly obvious to almost anyone you meet that you are kind, sympathetic and yet determined enough to stand up for anyone or anything that is truly important to you. Bright and sunny, you warm the world with your natural enthusiasm and would rarely do anything to hurt those around you, or at least not intentionally. In romance you are ardent and sincere, though some may find your style just a little overpowering. Gains come through your contacts with other people and this could be especially true with regard to romance, for love and money often come hand in hand for those who were born with Venus in Leo. People claim to understand you, though you are more complex than you seem.

Venus in Virgo

Your nature could well be fairly quiet no matter what your Sun sign might be, though this fact often manifests itself as an inner peace and would not prevent you from being basically sociable. Some delays and even the odd disappointment in love cannot be ruled out with this planetary position, though it's a fact that you will usually find the happiness you look for in the end. Catapulting yourself into romantic entanglements that you know to be rather ill-advised is not sensible, and it would be better to wait before you committed yourself exclusively to any one person. It is the essence of your nature to serve the world at large and through doing so it is possible that you will attract money at some stage in your life.

Venus in Libra

Venus is very comfortable in Libra and bestows upon those people who have this planetary position a particular sort of kindness that is easy to recognise. This is a very good position for all sorts of friendships and also for romantic attachments that usually bring much joy into your life. Few individuals with Venus in Libra would avoid marriage and since you are capable of great depths of love, it is likely that you will find a contented personal life. You like to mix with people of integrity and intelligence but don't take kindly to scruffy surroundings or work that means getting your hands too dirty. Careful speculation, good business dealings and money through marriage all seem fairly likely.

Venus in Scorpio

You are quite open and tend to spend money quite freely, even on those occasions when you don't have very much. Although your intentions are always good, there are times when you get yourself in to the odd scrape and this can be particularly true when it comes to romance, which you may come to late or from a rather unexpected direction. Certainly you have the power to be happy and to make others contented on the way, but you find the odd stumbling block on your journey through life and it could seem that you have to work harder than those around you. As a result of this, you gain a much deeper understanding of the true value of personal happiness than many people ever do, and are likely to achieve true contentment in the end.

Venus in Sagittarius

You are lighthearted, cheerful and always able to see the funny side of any situation. These facts enhance your popularity, which is especially high with members of the opposite sex. You should never have to look too far to find romantic interest in your life, though it is just possible that you might be too willing to commit yourself before you are certain that the person in question is right for you. Part of the problem here extends to other areas of life too. The fact is that you like variety in everything and so can tire of situations that fail to offer it. All the same, if you choose wisely and learn to understand your restless side, then great happiness can be yours.

Venus in Capricorn

The most notable trait that comes from Venus in this position is that it makes you trustworthy and able to take on all sorts of responsibilities in life. People are instinctively fond of you and love you all the more because you are always ready to help those who are in any form of need. Social and business popularity can be yours and there is a magnetic quality to your nature that is particularly attractive in a romantic sense. Anyone who wants a partner for a lover, a spouse and a good friend too would almost certainly look in your direction. Constancy is the hallmark of your nature and unfaithfulness would go right against the grain. You might sometimes be a little too trusting.

Venus in Aquarius

This location of Venus offers a fondness for travel and a desire to try out something new at every possible opportunity. You are extremely easy to get along with and tend to have many friends from varied backgrounds, classes and inclinations. You like to live a distinct sort of life and gain a great deal from moving about, both in a career sense and with regard to your home. It is not out of the question that you could form a romantic attachment to someone who comes from far away or be attracted to a person of a distinctly artistic and original nature. What you cannot stand is jealousy, for you have friends of both sexes and would want to keep things that way.

Venus in Pisces

The first thing people tend to notice about you is your wonderful, warm smile. Being very charitable by nature you will do anything to help others, even if you don't know them well. Much of your life may be spent sorting out situations for other people, but it is very important to feel that you are living for yourself too. In the main, you remain cheerful, and tend to be quite attractive to members of the opposite sex. Where romantic attachments are concerned, you could be drawn to people who are significantly older or younger than yourself or to someone with a unique career or point of view. It might be best for you to avoid marrying whilst you are still very young.

THE ASTRAL DIARY

HOW THE DIAGRAMS WORK

Through the picture diagrams in the Astral Diary I want to help you to plot your year. With them you can see where the positive and negative aspects will be found in each month. To make the most of them, all you have to do is remember where and when!

Let me show you how they work ...

THE MONTH AT A GLANCE

Just as there are twelve separate zodiac signs, so astrologers believe that each sign has twelve separate aspects to life. Each of the twelve segments relates to a different personal aspect. I list them all every month so that their meanings are always clear.

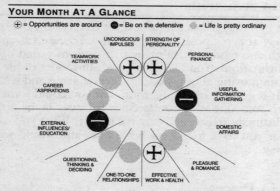

YOUR MONTH AT A GLANCE

⊕ = Opportunities are around   ⊖ = Be on the defensive   ◌ = Life is pretty ordinary

UNCONSCIOUS IMPULSES — STRENGTH OF PERSONALITY — PERSONAL FINANCE — USEFUL INFORMATION GATHERING — DOMESTIC AFFAIRS — PLEASURE & ROMANCE — EFFECTIVE WORK & HEALTH — ONE-TO-ONE RELATIONSHIPS — QUESTIONING, THINKING & DECIDING — EXTERNAL INFLUENCES/EDUCATION — CAREER ASPIRATIONS — TEAMWORK ACTIVITIES

I have designed this chart to show you how and when these twelve different aspects are being influenced throughout the year. When there is a shaded circle, nothing out of the ordinary is to be expected. However, when a circle turns white with a plus sign, the influence is positive. Where the circle is black with a minus sign, it is a negative.

YOUR ENERGY RHYTHM CHART

On the opposite page is a picture diagram in which I am linking your zodiac group to the rhythm of the Moon. In doing this I have calculated when you will be gaining strength from its influence and equally when you may be weakened by it.

If you think of yourself as being like the tides of the ocean then you may understand how your own energies must also rise and fall. And if you understand how it works and when it is working, then you can better organise your activities to achieve more and get things done more easily.

YOUR ENERGY RHYTHM CHART

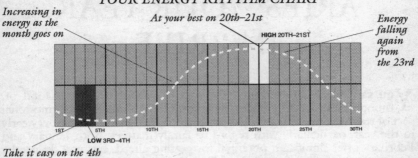

Increasing in energy as the month goes on

At your best on 20th–21st

HIGH 20TH–21ST

Energy falling again from the 23rd

1ST 5TH 10TH 15TH 20TH 25TH 30TH

LOW 3RD–4TH

Take it easy on the 4th

MOVING PICTURE SCREEN
Love, money, career and vitality measured every week

The diagram at the end of each week is designed to be informative and fun. The arrows move up and down the scale to give you an idea of the strength of your opportunities in each area. If LOVE stands at plus 4, then get out and put yourself about because things are going your way in romance! The further down the arrow goes, the weaker the opportunities. Do note that the diagram is an overall view of your astrological aspects and therefore reflects a trend which may not concur with every day in that cycle.

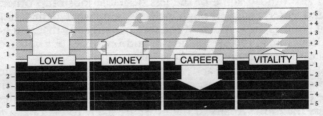

LOVE   MONEY   CAREER   VITALITY

AND FINALLY:

am ....

pm ....

The two lines that are left blank in each daily entry of the Astral Diary are for your own personal use. You may find them ideal for keeping a check on birthdays or appointments, though it could be an idea to make notes from the astrological trends and diagrams a few weeks in advance. Some of the lines are marked with a key, which indicates the working of astrological cycles in your life. Look out for them each week as they are the best days to take action or make decisions. The daily text tells you which area of your life to focus on.

☿ = Mercury is retrograde on that day.

ARIES: YOUR YEAR
IN BRIEF

You can expect pretty much the sort of year that Aries is fond of, though there are differences, most noticeably a much more emotional sort of response under many circumstances. This is obvious even very early in the year, particularly with regard to family matters. Both January and February offer significant potential for getting ahead, but you do need a degree of circumspection and to fall back upon your previous experience on occasions. This is not always easy for a sign such as yours.

As March comes along, so you are concentrating very hard on getting ahead in a practical and financial sense, so much so that the niceties of life tend to take a back seat. April is similar, though more balanced and offering new incentives that positively demand your co-operation with others. The world seems to expand at this time and you will also be addressing personal matters in a very adult manner.

May finds you with exciting prospects before you, with a summer that looks potentially rewarding. If rules and regulations get on your nerves, you should be able to find ways to circumnavigate them to a large degree and can also offload some of the less desirable jobs onto others. June is active and enterprising, though perhaps somewhat demanding from a financial point of view. Much of the summer suggests that you need to be careful how much you are spending, and on what, but you are resilient and can easily earn more when necessary.

The months of July and August find you in the middle of new enterprises, both in a professional and a social sense. Mixing business with pleasure ought to be a piece of cake and you have plenty of energy when it matters the most. Affairs of the heart are likely to be a main feature of your life, with new relationships for some. Travel tends to be important. This is less obvious with the arrival of the autumn, if only because you have so much to do. Practical matters are most significant and remain so throughout September and October.

November proves interesting and varied, with gains coming in from unexpected directions. Your sense of proportion is good, as is your ability to get on with a wealth of different sorts of people. Avoid arguing for your limitations, as others may believe you. November is followed by a spectacular December, at least up to Christmas, when things slow markedly. Some patience is required between December 25th and the end of the year, though with careful handling, even this time can be productive and happy.

January
2005

YOUR MONTH AT A GLANCE

⊕ = Opportunities are around   ⊖ = Be on the defensive   ⬤ = Life is pretty ordinary

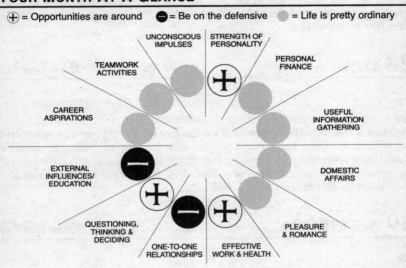

- UNCONSCIOUS IMPULSES
- STRENGTH OF PERSONALITY
- TEAMWORK ACTIVITIES
- PERSONAL FINANCE
- CAREER ASPIRATIONS
- USEFUL INFORMATION GATHERING
- EXTERNAL INFLUENCES/ EDUCATION
- DOMESTIC AFFAIRS
- QUESTIONING, THINKING & DECIDING
- ONE-TO-ONE RELATIONSHIPS
- EFFECTIVE WORK & HEALTH
- PLEASURE & ROMANCE

JANUARY HIGHS AND LOWS

Here I show you how the rhythms of the Moon will affect you this month. Like the tide, your energies and abilities will rise and fall with its pattern. When it is above the centre line, go for it, when it is below, you should be resting.

HIGH 15TH–17TH

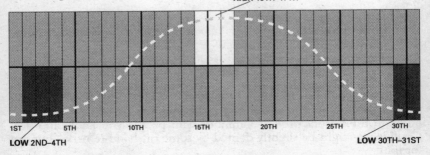

1ST   5TH   10TH   15TH   20TH   25TH   30TH

LOW 2ND–4TH

LOW 30TH–31ST

27 MONDAY

Moon Age Day 16   Moon Sign Cancer

am . . . .

pm . . . .
Mars enters your solar ninth house, causing you to feel it is time to broaden some of your horizons. If you are away from work until the New Year you will have the time to think about such matters. Socially speaking, you will probably be happy to stick to those people you know best, for today at least.

28 TUESDAY

Moon Age Day 17   Moon Sign Leo

am . . . .

pm . . . .
You can learn something new and exciting now. Keep your ears open and be willing to alter your plans at the last minute in order to achieve something splendid. It's turning out to be a hectic and effective period between Christmas and the New Year, but don't forget that part of the reason for holidays is to have a rest.

29 WEDNESDAY

Moon Age Day 18   Moon Sign Leo

am . . . .

pm . . . .
A strong emphasis now shows on leisure and pleasure – probably not a moment too soon. In a more practical sense you will simply have to be patient. There is nothing to be gained right now from rushing your fences and there are so few people at work this week some of your offers would be wasted.

30 THURSDAY

Moon Age Day 19   Moon Sign Virgo

am . . . .

pm . . . .
Getting things done efficiently is uppermost in your mind today. That's fine, but remember the advice of yesterday. Better by far to spend a few hours in the bosom of your family or with people you know and like. Confidence might be slightly dented by some off-hand remarks, but not for long.

31 FRIDAY
Moon Age Day 20   Moon Sign Virgo

am . . . .

pm . . . .
Your social life ought to prove quite rewarding. Creative potential is good and you may have decided to make some sort of change at home. As long as it is something that makes you more comfortable, and not less so, then your efforts are worthwhile. Let someone else undertake a domestic task.

1 SATURDAY
Moon Age Day 21   Moon Sign Virgo

am . . . .

pm . . . .
The first day of the year offers you a unique opportunity to get something timely done, before others have a chance to beat you to the punch. There are gains to be made in several different directions, even though you might feel as though there is general lethargy being shown by those who matter the most.

2 SUNDAY
Moon Age Day 22   Moon Sign Libra

am . . . .

pm . . . .
Venus is in your solar ninth house, which for you means beneficial trends surrounding mental pursuits and personal freedom. You are strong in nature and quite able to let others know how you feel about almost anything. What you do need as the lunar low arrives is reassurance and the knowledge that the one you love is on your side.

3 MONDAY
Moon Age Day 23   Moon Sign Libra

am . . . .

pm . . . .
If you are not feeling on top form today, perhaps you can blame the presence of the lunar low. Your best response is to keep yourself to yourself and concentrate on jobs you are sure about. It won't be long before you are bursting with vitality again but for the moment you may have little choice but to go with the flow.

4 TUESDAY
Moon Age Day 24   Moon Sign Libra

am . . . .

pm . . . .
Vitality might still be in short supply, which is why you would be best advised to stick to what you know and stay away from innovations of almost any sort. You would be wise to keep a tight hold on money and save any real spending until later in the week, by which time you will have a sounder head on your shoulders.

5 WEDNESDAY
Moon Age Day 25   Moon Sign Scorpio

am . . . .

pm . . . .
Getting out and about is now clearly far more rewarding. You are in a good position to get what you want, particularly in a romantic sense. The attitude of a friend might puzzle you somewhat and it would be sensible to ask a few leading questions before you fire from the hip, as Aries people are inclined to do.

6 THURSDAY
Moon Age Day 26   Moon Sign Scorpio

am . . . .

pm . . . .
Pleasantries from a social point of view are now far more likely. If you have to do anything that goes against the grain, and especially if it's something that crops up regularly, try to change your attitude towards it. You can make a pleasure out of a chore if you only approach it from the right direction.

7 FRIDAY
Moon Age Day 27   Moon Sign Sagittarius

am . . . .

pm . . . .
You show great dynamism right now, particularly with regard to your career. If you are a student, you could find that your studies come very easily to you at the moment, and virtually all Aries people will be monitoring a very definite improvement in terms of personal popularity. Don't be surprised if someone wants to know you better.

8 SATURDAY
Moon Age Day 28   Moon Sign Sagittarius

am . . . .

pm . . . .
This is a weekend of comings and goings and you will be included amongst them. Actually getting to grips with anything much might be hard, but you show a very definite face to the world and it is unlikely that anyone would be taking you for granted. Stick at something you know to be important.

9 SUNDAY
Moon Age Day 29   Moon Sign Capricorn

am . . . .

pm . . . .
You may have got out of the habit of a particular task or set of jobs that you know to be very important. This Sunday offers you the chance to look at them again and to get on side with a person who hasn't been very easy to deal with of late. You will be amazed at just how much you can get done.

10 MONDAY
Moon Age Day 0   Moon Sign Capricorn

am . . . .

pm . . . .
This is still a very favourable time when it comes to social developments
of almost any sort. There are also some financial gains possible at the start
of this week, together with the chance to make the very best impression
on someone who could turn out to be very important in your life.

11 TUESDAY
Moon Age Day 1   Moon Sign Aquarius

am . . . .

pm . . . .
Getting yourself organised is what life is really about today. Confidence
is high and you are able to tell the whole world what you want, and how
you intend to go about getting it. There may be necessary changes in the
pipeline, but this is no time to by shying away from any of them.

12 WEDNESDAY
Moon Age Day 2   Moon Sign Aquarius

am . . . .

pm . . . .
Your ability to attract just the right sort of company is well emphasised at
this time, so make the most of it. Following your intuition, you can also
call upon the support of people who have not only influence but real
power. If someone is bothering you, now is the time to tell them the way
things really are.

13 THURSDAY
Moon Age Day 3   Moon Sign Pisces

am . . . .

pm . . . .
Your mental processes are sharp and get better the more you find yourself
in open discussion with others. The real Aries grit is evident and it is
highly unlikely that anyone will get in your way. Something you have
been looking forward to might not prove quite as interesting or
rewarding as you had hoped.

14 FRIDAY

Moon Age Day 4   Moon Sign Pisces

am . . . .

pm . . . .
There is a brief time of withdrawal ahead of the lunar high, which is why you may decide to spend far more time today listening than talking. Someone you haven't seen for ages may be making a repeat appearance in your life, bringing with them a few stark realities, but also some interesting possibilities.

15 SATURDAY

Moon Age Day 5   Moon Sign Aries

am . . . .

pm . . . .
As the lunar high arrives, look around carefully because nobody is better at making the best of opportunities than you are right now. Not everything you want will be forthcoming, but when it isn't, you may simply have yourself to blame. In the best of all worlds, you will usually only have to ask for what you want before it comes your way.

16 SUNDAY

Moon Age Day 6   Moon Sign Aries

am . . . .

pm . . . .
Getting others round to your way of thinking should be an absolute piece of cake right now, which is why you have scope to get on so well. There might be someone about who you don't trust. However, your intuition is so strong at the moment that it is unlikely you would have the wool pulled over your eyes.

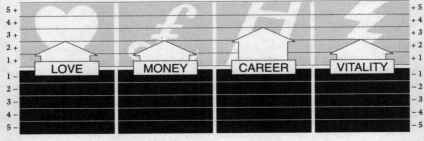

17 MONDAY

Moon Age Day 7   Moon Sign Aries

am ....

pm ....
Anything you hear right now in connection with your work is well worth mulling over carefully. You don't generally listen too much to gossip, but it might be worthwhile doing so for the next couple of days. The deeper and more spiritual side of Aries is now on display, which might surprise a few people.

18 TUESDAY

Moon Age Day 8   Moon Sign Taurus

am ....

pm ....
The planetary focus is once again on your career, or studies if you are in full-time education. You concentrate very well now and can easily get ahead of the competition, simply by showing the world what you are made of. If this means speaking out, then that is what you must do.

19 WEDNESDAY

Moon Age Day 9   Moon Sign Taurus

am ....

pm ....
A continued boost to all matters professional is the gift of the present position of the Sun. Even if there is time to enjoy yourself, in all probability you will be far too preoccupied with other matters. During a period when you can attract money, there might be little enough time to spend it.

20 THURSDAY

Moon Age Day 10   Moon Sign Gemini

am ....

pm ....
When it comes to any sort of practical task, it appears you have all the help you could possibly need today. Of course, you might have to open your mouth and say what you need, but that doesn't come at all hard to you. Concentrate on the most important matters early in the day and enjoy yourself later.

21 FRIDAY
Moon Age Day 11   Moon Sign Gemini

am . . . .

pm . . . .
The Sun now enters your solar eleventh house, enabling you to become a much better team operator than has been the case since Christmas. Listen carefully to what other people have to say and don't get too carried away with your own opinions. You might be surprised how much there is to learn.

22 SATURDAY
Moon Age Day 12   Moon Sign Cancer

am . . . .

pm . . . .
A rather busy phase at work might leave you too stressed to take full advantage of some of the opportunities that the weekend offers. Maybe you are bringing your work home with you, or else thinking about it so much that you simply fail to register many of the offers and opportunities that come your way socially.

23 SUNDAY
Moon Age Day 13   Moon Sign Cancer

am . . . .

pm . . . .
Mars in your solar ninth house indicates that you should avoid alienating the very people who are in the best position to lend you a timely hand. There may be chores about that you don't relish. All the more reason to get them out of the way as soon as you can, before you settle down to good times and romance.

24 MONDAY
Moon Age Day 14   Moon Sign Cancer

am . . . .

pm . . . .
Trends indicate that there are gains coming your way, even if you are not particularly looking for them. What should work out well for you at present is listening to the advice of people you really rate. On the other hand, you will probably be staying right away from individuals you find tedious or tiresome.

25 TUESDAY
Moon Age Day 15   Moon Sign Leo

am . . . .

pm . . . .
A day to listen to what your friends are saying because they are making great sense. A long-lost buddy could well come back into your life and could bring a new opportunity with them. It isn't out of the question that you will be replaying an old issue, only this time working it to your genuine advantage.

26 WEDNESDAY
Moon Age Day 16   Moon Sign Leo

am . . . .

pm . . . .
You have scope to explore your more creative side at present and to use the position of the Moon to express your innermost thoughts and feelings. Even Aries can't be on the go all the time, which is why it might be sensible to take a break if one is offered. Money could be coming from unexpected places.

27 THURSDAY
Moon Age Day 17   Moon Sign Virgo

am . . . .

pm . . . .
Present influences might well make it very easy for you to do things, which could be something of a curse if others accuse you of being too smart for your own good. All the same, you need to plough your own furrow, even if this means getting on the wrong side of someone who is really important to you.

28 FRIDAY
Moon Age Day 18   Moon Sign Virgo

am . . . .

pm . . . .
If you find you are becoming involved in too many arguments today, you could have yourself to blame. The likelihood is you know what you want but could be rather too dominant in the way you choose to go about getting it. A little tact and diplomacy could go a long way ahead of the weekend and all it offers.

29 SATURDAY
Moon Age Day 19   Moon Sign Virgo

am . . . .

pm . . . .
There are rewarding times in store and all you really have to do to make the most of them is to be in the right place at the right time. Intuition helps again, leading to a weekend that offers a great deal of variety and the chance to make impressions on people who could prove to be important later.

30 SUNDAY
Moon Age Day 20   Moon Sign Libra

am . . . .

pm . . . .
Progress could now slow, as the lunar low inclines you to stand and watch, rather than getting involved to the extent you might normally wish. If there is an opportunity to get ahead, this is born out of patience and thought, rather than action. Such a period probably goes against the grain as far as you are concerned.

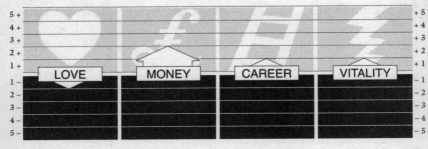

31 MONDAY
Moon Age Day 21   Moon Sign Libra

am . . . .

pm . . . .
Don't take all the world's troubles onto your own shoulders. You will get ahead far better if you take things steadily and deal with issues that arise one at a time. Romance could be the best place to look for comfort and reassurance at the moment, even if you find yourself in the arms of someone rather surprising.

1 TUESDAY
Moon Age Day 22   Moon Sign Scorpio

am . . . .

pm . . . .
Group and co-operative matters work distinctly to your advantage at the start of February. Creative potential is especially good and you can explore it best when in the company of people you find to be both stimulating and interesting. Confusion could well follow if you try to be too tactful for your own good.

2 WEDNESDAY
Moon Age Day 23   Moon Sign Scorpio

am . . . .

pm . . . .
If you take chances today, choose them carefully. Risks are fine, just as long as they are calculated. Aries is sometimes inclined to push matters just for the sake of doing so, though behaving in this manner at the moment won't get you very far at all, and might lead to a degree of confusion you could do without.

3 THURSDAY
Moon Age Day 24   Moon Sign Scorpio

am . . . .

pm . . . .
An argumentative tendency, thanks to the present position of Mars in your solar chart, could get you into a degree of trouble. Your best approach is to listen to what others have to say and then react calmly. In the end, you will be pleased that you kept your temper and that you avoided unnecessary arguments and confusion.

4 FRIDAY   *Moon Age Day 25   Moon Sign Sagittarius*

am ....

pm ....
You may well want to be a freewheeler today, though it might not be too easy. There is a long way to go in a particular issue, which is why it would be very sensible to hold back for a while. You should not have to look too far to find romance. It might be around the next corner, or even within your own home environment.

5 SATURDAY   *Moon Age Day 26   Moon Sign Sagittarius*

am ....

pm ....
Venus in your solar eleventh house inspires social highlights and a genuine desire to do what comes naturally. Others find you to be very interesting and entertaining and you barely have to open your mouth in order to find fans streaming in from all directions. The strange thing is, you won't be surprised.

6 SUNDAY   *Moon Age Day 27   Moon Sign Capricorn*

am ....

pm ....
Even if you can't presently bring everyone round to your way of thinking, the people who matter the most are already on your side. There might be a good deal of dashing about this Sunday, but on the way there ought to be good opportunities for enjoyment and for getting to know someone much better.

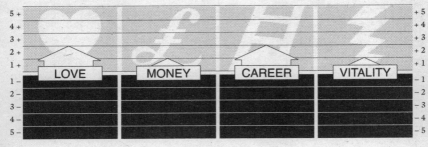

February 2005

YOUR MONTH AT A GLANCE

⊕ = Opportunities are around   ⊖ = Be on the defensive   ⬤ = Life is pretty ordinary

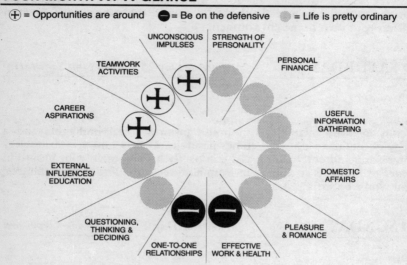

FEBRUARY HIGHS AND LOWS

Here I show you how the rhythms of the Moon will affect you this month. Like the tide, your energies and abilities will rise and fall with its pattern. When it is above the centre line, go for it, when it is below, you should be resting.

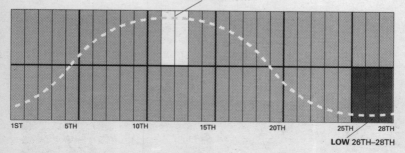

7 MONDAY
Moon Age Day 28   Moon Sign Capricorn

am . . . .

pm . . . .
Today could be quite sluggish in a professional sense, which is why you are now much more likely to rely on the help and support of those around you. Now is the time to concentrate on matters that you know to be of supreme importance and leave the dross until another day. In your spare moments, you might choose to read.

8 TUESDAY
Moon Age Day 29   Moon Sign Aquarius

am . . . .

pm . . . .
Major powers are now on the ascendant again and you are in a position to make the best of any opportunity that comes your way. This could be a good time on the romantic front and you have what it takes to show a positive face in friendship. Concern for colleagues is well marked and you will offer timely help.

9 WEDNESDAY
Moon Age Day 0   Moon Sign Aquarius

am . . . .

pm . . . .
Today's greatest source of joy and pleasure comes from your association with those around you. This could be at work or maybe once you are finished with the daily round. Sensitive and caring, you show the warmest side of Aries and will be particularly concerned to support the underdog.

10 THURSDAY
Moon Age Day 1   Moon Sign Pisces

am . . . .

pm . . . .
Trends suggest that group encounters interest you greatly, though you might have to reorder your schedule somewhat in order to get the best from them. If you don't have time to do everything that seems to be necessary, you could try delegating. This isn't always easy for your zodiac sign, but is sometimes necessary.

11 FRIDAY

Moon Age Day 2   Moon Sign Pisces

am . . . .

pm . . . .
General routines have the ability to distract you from ideas you know to be revolutionary and stimulating. Once again, it is very necessary to look carefully at what the day requires and to leave alone those jobs that are not at all necessary. A day to avoid becoming bored at all costs, and when assessing others, to use your intuition.

12 SATURDAY

Moon Age Day 3   Moon Sign Aries

am . . . .

pm . . . .
With the lunar high offering a marked boost to your personal energies, this weekend could prove to be the best so far this year. Although the winter weather might prevent you from going far, you will still be in the mood to travel if you can. Aries is the most intrepid of all the zodiac signs, and you can show the fact at present.

13 SUNDAY

Moon Age Day 4   Moon Sign Aries

am . . . .

pm . . . .
A word in the right ear could go a long way to getting you what you want from life. The lunar high presents you with new and better chances to get ahead and you show a preference for people who are very similar in nature to yourself. There is just the slightest chance that you prove contrary in personal matters.

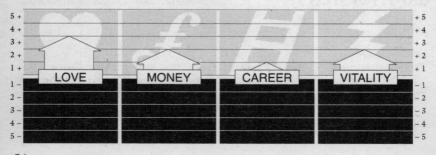

14 MONDAY
Moon Age Day 5   Moon Sign Taurus

am . . . .

pm . . . .
A dynamic approach to personal matters once again displays itself at the start of a new working week. If you have been toiling away during the weekend, you will be in a better position to see what you really should be doing. If not, getting yourself fully into gear is likely to take a little time.

15 TUESDAY
Moon Age Day 6   Moon Sign Taurus

am . . . .

pm . . . .
You should be doing your very best to establish new social contacts this week, and today is as good a time as any to get started. When it comes to words of love, you are able to dredge more up than an 18th-century poet. This is unusual behaviour for Aries, so you could shock your partner or someone else dear to your heart.

16 WEDNESDAY
Moon Age Day 7   Moon Sign Gemini

am . . . .

pm . . . .
If there are plans of action around you that prove difficult to follow, you need to swallow your pride and simply ask. You might find this to be a slightly humbling experience, which is never easy for your zodiac sign. Go ahead; it's possible that people will be only too willing to let you in on their secrets.

17 THURSDAY
Moon Age Day 8   Moon Sign Gemini

am . . . .

pm . . . .
Your mental strengths may not exactly be up to par at present, which means you may have to take things somewhat steadily at the moment. Mercury is now entering your solar twelfth house and you benefit from quiet contemplation and even outright meditation, if you can convince yourself to indulge in such a pastime.

18 FRIDAY

Moon Age Day 9   Moon Sign Gemini

am . . . .

pm . . . .
Maybe you should not try too hard to gain the ear of colleagues or to influence the outcome of specific events today. The chances are that you are still not firing on all cylinders and would gain from a short period of limited isolation. You might decide to curl up somewhere with a good book, or better still with some sort of puzzle.

19 SATURDAY

Moon Age Day 10   Moon Sign Cancer

am . . . .

pm . . . .
The signs are that the pressure is now on again in a professional sense, and you are never quiet for more than a couple of days. There are matters around that interest you greatly and you simply cannot wait to show the world at large what you are made of. Comfort and security are probably now the last things on your mind.

20 SUNDAY

Moon Age Day 11   Moon Sign Cancer

am . . . .

pm . . . .
The Sun, now in your solar twelfth house, might make it somewhat difficult to get ahead in quite the way you would wish. There are lingering feelings that people are not pulling for you, though the problem, if there is one, may be of your own invention. Try to be as relaxed as possible.

21 MONDAY
Moon Age Day 12   Moon Sign Leo

am . . . .

pm . . . .
You have potential to be very entertaining company at present. The fact is that you are outgoing enough to be fun, yet can show a really sensitive side that others don't always see and which they really like. Confidence could be somewhat lacking, especially if there are important decisions that simply have to be made.

22 TUESDAY
Moon Age Day 13   Moon Sign Leo

am . . . .

pm . . . .
When it comes to professional matters, you are able to fire on all cylinders at present and show the world what you are made of. However, it is important that you do not lose sight of the bigger picture in a personal sense, so you would be wise to listen to what loved ones are saying once your working commitment is out of the way.

23 WEDNESDAY
Moon Age Day 14   Moon Sign Leo

am . . . .

pm . . . .
Pleasant experiences on the social front make for an entertaining time and should leave you feeling that life is more than worthwhile. Unfortunately, not everyone is in quite the frame of mind that you are and a degree of patience may be necessary when dealing with folk who simply won't be happy.

24 THURSDAY
Moon Age Day 15   Moon Sign Virgo

am . . . .

pm . . . .
A brief astrological trend could leave you somewhat muddle-headed today, which is why it would not be sensible to make too many decisions if you can possibly avoid doing so. Routines are on your mind, even if you try to shirk them, and it might be better to simply get them out of the way, leaving the decks cleared for action.

25 FRIDAY

Moon Age Day 16   Moon Sign Virgo

am . . . .

pm . . . .
Don't be surprised if not all your ambitions are working out quite as you
would have wished. It is very important to deal with situations as they
arise. If you do so, it is quite possible to make positive strides, even
against prevailing circumstances. Above all, show yourself to be as flexible
as possible.

26 SATURDAY

Moon Age Day 17   Moon Sign Libra

am . . . .

pm . . . .
Enthusiasm could well be lacking and there isn't much you can do about
the situation. The lunar low has potential to sap your strength and
resolve, leaving you feeling you have little choice but to go with the flow.
Why not leave important decisions until later and content yourself with
what you have at the moment?

27 SUNDAY

Moon Age Day 18   Moon Sign Libra

am . . . .

pm . . . .
Definitely another day during which you should slow down and take
things one at a time. There is absolutely no point in rushing because all
that will happen is that you will get yourself into a terrible state. A better
option is to allow others to make the running and be willing to let them
organise what you should be doing.

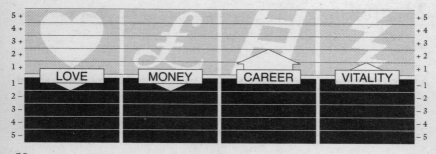

28 MONDAY
Moon Age Day 19   Moon Sign Libra

am . . . .

pm . . . .
The third day on which trends may hinder your progress. The lunar low is definitely having a bearing on your thinking and actions and so a contemplative period is indicated. However, there is nothing at all to prevent you from laying down plans you can begin to implement as early as tomorrow.

1 TUESDAY
Moon Age Day 20   Moon Sign Scorpio

am . . . .

pm . . . .
The first day of March ought to prove much more rewarding than of late. It is towards intimate relationships that you are presently encouraged to turn your gaze and it seems as though you have a great deal of influence regarding the thoughts and actions of loved ones. Money-wise, joint matters could be on your mind at the moment.

2 WEDNESDAY
Moon Age Day 21   Moon Sign Scorpio

am . . . .

pm . . . .
Although your influence is just a little limited whilst the Sun remains in your solar twelfth house, you are still able to get ahead, using a combination of careful planning and wise actions. Pick on the best people in your vicinity to lend a hand when you know it would be providential to do so.

3 THURSDAY
Moon Age Day 22   Moon Sign Sagittarius

am . . . .

pm . . . .
This is definitely the best time to broaden your personal horizons. You can do this by carefully watching what is going on around you. Many of the ideas you have are probably a great deal better than those of people around you. Convincing them that you know best ought to be a piece of cake if you remain calm.

4 FRIDAY
Moon Age Day 23   Moon Sign Sagittarius

am . . . .

pm . . . .
Romantically speaking today could be something of a downer, though if you are aware of the fact, you can deal with it quite easily. Don't get into too many clinches, particularly if to do so means raising the jealousy of someone else. You might prefer to keep your contacts light and casual for the present time.

5 SATURDAY
Moon Age Day 24   Moon Sign Capricorn

am . . . .

pm . . . .
Slowly but surely your practical skills are beginning to show themselves more fully. Step by careful step, you are able to get ahead and to convince those around you that you know what you are doing. In terms of money, now is the time to begin taking the odd chance, because calculated risks could well pay off.

6 SUNDAY
Moon Age Day 25   Moon Sign Capricorn

am . . . .

pm . . . .
There are serious decisions to be taken at the moment and not all of them are instantly recognisable. Some deep thought is required and you certainly cannot afford to shoot from the hip in the way that Aries is sometimes inclined to do. If necessary, seek out the help of someone who is a consummate professional in their own field.

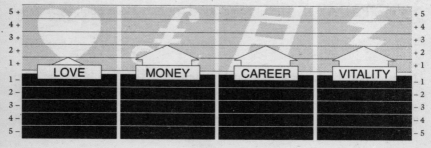

March 2005

YOUR MONTH AT A GLANCE

⊕ = Opportunities are around   ⊖ = Be on the defensive   ● = Life is pretty ordinary

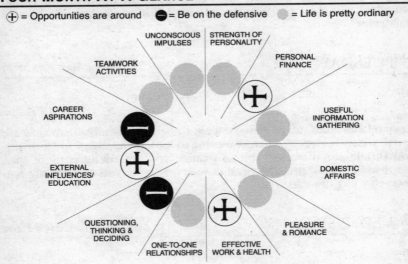

UNCONSCIOUS IMPULSES

STRENGTH OF PERSONALITY

TEAMWORK ACTIVITIES

PERSONAL FINANCE

CAREER ASPIRATIONS

USEFUL INFORMATION GATHERING

EXTERNAL INFLUENCES/ EDUCATION

DOMESTIC AFFAIRS

QUESTIONING, THINKING & DECIDING

PLEASURE & ROMANCE

ONE-TO-ONE RELATIONSHIPS

EFFECTIVE WORK & HEALTH

MARCH HIGHS AND LOWS

Here I show you how the rhythms of the Moon will affect you this month. Like the tide, your energies and abilities will rise and fall with its pattern. When it is above the centre line, go for it, when it is below, you should be resting.

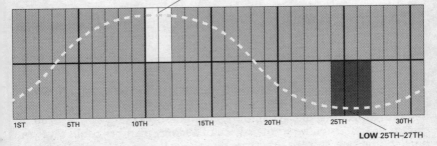

HIGH 11TH–12TH

LOW 25TH–27TH

1ST   5TH   10TH   15TH   20TH   25TH   30TH

61

7 MONDAY
Moon Age Day 26   Moon Sign Aquarius

am . . . .

pm . . . .
Trends suggest that a social contact might let you down, though friends
you have known for ages are much less likely to cause you problems. You
need to choose your associates very carefully at the moment and should
not allow sentiment to get in the way of decisions you know to by very
important.

8 TUESDAY
Moon Age Day 27   Moon Sign Aquarius

am . . . .

pm . . . .
Love relationships might actually seem to be more trouble than they are
worth today. However, when you come to look at the situation rationally,
you should see that every bit of trouble you are taking is more than
worthwhile. Look after the pennies today, because you could easily find
yourself short of cash.

9 WEDNESDAY
Moon Age Day 28   Moon Sign Pisces

am . . . .

pm . . . .
Your powers and influence may be somewhat limited today, just ahead of
the lunar high. You might have to let others make some of the running
and take a few of the necessary decisions. There are tasks around that you
simply don't want to do, but a degree of self-discipline is clearly called for
at this time.

10 THURSDAY
Moon Age Day 0   Moon Sign Pisces

am . . . .

pm . . . .
Unlike yesterday, you now have what it takes to be much more fired up
in a professional sense. This is a time during which you are looking
forward to getting ahead, and the amount of work you can shift is
extraordinary. Listening to the advice of a family member could save you
time and money, so keep your ears open.

11 FRIDAY
Moon Age Day 1   Moon Sign Aries

am . . . .

pm . . . .

The Moon returns to your zodiac sign and brings Lady Luck along with it. Although you will fight shy of taking unnecessary risks, there are great gains to be made through taking some chances. Your powers of communication are especially well marked and it seems as though you cannot put a foot wrong.

12 SATURDAY
Moon Age Day 2   Moon Sign Aries

am . . . .

pm . . . .

The more ambitious you choose to be today, the better things are likely to go for you. There may be moments when you feel as though you could rule the world, though of course this is illusion, so a degree of realism is also called for. Socially speaking, you can make the most favourable of impressions.

13 SUNDAY
Moon Age Day 3   Moon Sign Taurus

am . . . .

pm . . . .

Today has potential to be both busy and interesting. If you have to do things that go against the grain, you should discover that even this offers a degree of interest you didn't expect. Contributing to the success of others is something that ought to appeal, even though this isn't a typical Aries trait.

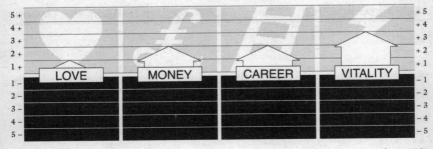

14 MONDAY

Moon Age Day 4   Moon Sign Taurus

am . . . .

pm . . . .
A period of your life comes along in which you may be feeling somewhat
negative, particularly about romantic attachments. The likelihood is that
you need a degree of change, perhaps because you are feeling somehow
isolated. Digging up old contacts from the past might appeal, though it
appears that you are generally restless right now.

15 TUESDAY

Moon Age Day 5   Moon Sign Taurus

am . . . .

pm . . . .
You might find you are unable to cope if you take on too many
responsibilities at this time. Settling into a routine rarely does appeal to
you, and the winter may seem to be dragging on forever at this point in
time. Why not stay away from major responsibilities and find ways in
which to enjoy yourself if you can?

16 WEDNESDAY

Moon Age Day 6   Moon Sign Gemini

am . . . .

pm . . . .
You can now put some of your versatility to use, particularly in a work
sense. When you are away from the professional arena, you should notice
that personal attachments seem somewhat more rewarding and offer you
incentives to be as kind as you can be to someone who really counts in
your life.

17 THURSDAY

Moon Age Day 7   Moon Sign Gemini

am . . . .

pm . . . .
Another mental peak comes along as little Mercury consolidates its
position in your solar first house. Your intellect is honed to perfection,
enabling you to turn heads wherever you go. This is Aries at its very best,
and there is no doubt that you are a force to be reckoned with.

18 FRIDAY

Moon Age Day 8   Moon Sign Cancer

am . . . .

pm . . . .
Although you are still generally interested in life, events in and around
your home might prove less than inspiring. Maybe you need a break and
to be in the company of people who get your juices flowing. Set yourself
some sort of challenge; that's a strategy that generally works if Aries is
becoming bored.

19 SATURDAY

Moon Age Day 9   Moon Sign Cancer

am . . . .

pm . . . .
Recent ideas and initiatives come back into your mind, perhaps because
Saturday offers you a chance to look at things in greater detail. Try not
to count every tedious step in a job you simply do not want to do. Good
times are there for the taking, though for the moment you might be
forgiven for missing the fact.

20 SUNDAY   ☿

Moon Age Day 10   Moon Sign Cancer

am . . . .

pm . . . .
The Sun enters your solar first house, an event that your nature has been
crying out for across the last few days. Initiatives are greater in number
and you can put yourself at the leading edge of whatever is happening in
your vicinity. Remember to take things steadily, however, because this is
a Sunday and relaxation is called for.

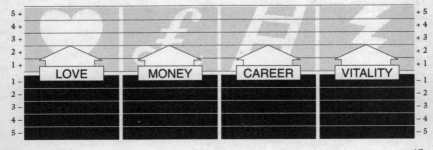

21 MONDAY ☿ *Moon Age Day 11   Moon Sign Leo*

am . . . .

pm . . . .
You can now be the star attraction in a social sense, at the beginning of
a new working week that has a great deal to offer you. There are signs
that you put extra effort into those jobs you really favour, maybe at the
expense of tasks you don't really want to undertake at all. This is a
recurring theme during March, and has to be guarded against.

22 TUESDAY ☿ *Moon Age Day 12   Moon Sign Leo*

am . . . .

pm . . . .
If you want a day during which it is possible to get your own way most
of the time, this could be it. You should remember not to be selfish,
though, because it would be all too easy to make an enemy if you push
forward with all those Aries guns blazing. Your general attitude is good,
especially in personal attachments.

23 WEDNESDAY ☿ *Moon Age Day 13   Moon Sign Virgo*

am . . . .

pm . . . .
Even if you are now clearly enjoying the mental challenges that life has
to offer, there are times when it will be difficult to fit in everything you
really want to do. The secret is to plan ahead and to take on those social
demands that interest you the most. It is the undertones of what loved
ones are saying that you notice the most.

24 THURSDAY ☿ *Moon Age Day 14   Moon Sign Virgo*

am . . . .

pm . . . .
It is possible that your sights will have to be set somewhat lower, because
it appears you are making demands on yourself that are just too great. Of
course, Aries is capable of almost anything, but you are still human. If
you burn the candle at both ends indefinitely, exhaustion is going to be
the result.

25 FRIDAY ☿ *Moon Age Day 15   Moon Sign Libra*

am . . . .

pm . . . .
The lunar low encourages you to slow down and to take account of the fact that your juices are not flowing as freely at this time of the month. Confidence is not lacking, but decisions of a very important nature are probably best left until a future date. The end of the working week might offer scope for a financial bonus.

26 SATURDAY ☿ *Moon Age Day 16   Moon Sign Libra*

am . . . .

pm . . . .
You are easily defeated by life under present influences, which is strange for your zodiac sign. This could mean that others will notice and will do all they can to boost your spirits. Keep to quiet pursuits and to those interests that take your mind off worries that have no real substance. Confidence returns soon, but for now simply plod along.

27 SUNDAY ☿ *Moon Age Day 17   Moon Sign Libra*

am . . . .

pm . . . .
Another reasonably quiet day, though you can see the light at the end of the tunnel and may be planning future strategy. This would be a good time to settle down with a book or to watch a film that has always inspired you. Intellectually speaking you are on top form, though getting your message across is the potential problem.

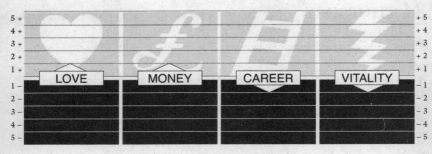

28 MONDAY ☿ *Moon Age Day 18   Moon Sign Scorpio*

am . . . .

pm . . . .
A lift to your love life comes along as the weekend disappears into the background. The lunar low is left behind and all opportunities now look crisper and sharper than has been the case of late. With a degree of excitement you can't really explain, there are significant gains to be made around every new corner.

29 TUESDAY ☿ *Moon Age Day 19   Moon Sign Scorpio*

am . . . .

pm . . . .
If progress has been lacking of late, and it almost certainly has, now is the time to push forward with all the strength you can muster. You need to get your teeth into new projects and should not be suffering for any sort of lethargy, particularly in the professional world. Even personal attachments should look better.

30 WEDNESDAY ☿ *Moon Age Day 20   Moon Sign Sagittarius*

am . . . .

pm . . . .
You have what it takes to keep up a varied and highly stimulating love life right now. Typical of you, there are not enough hours in a day to fit in everything you would wish to do, but if you are selective you should discover possibilities that had not occurred to you before. You may be able to strengthen finances around now.

31 THURSDAY ☿ *Moon Age Day 21   Moon Sign Sagittarius*

am . . . .

pm . . . .
Now is the time to lay down plans for the forthcoming weekend and make sure they include something you enjoy doing, even if it doesn't provide any particular gain in a financial sense. Life is not all about money, a fact that becomes obvious around now. Look carefully at the way certain people are approaching you.

YOUR DAILY GUIDE TO APRIL 2005

1 FRIDAY ☿ *Moon Age Day 22   Moon Sign Capricorn*

am . . . .

pm . . . .
A new month dawns and you are potentially in such a good frame of
mind that you won't care at all if people play the odd April Fool joke on
you. Aries can be humorous and even silly on occasions, which shows
quite markedly now. People like you, and it's a great feeling to know that
you are number one in someone's chart.

2 SATURDAY ☿ *Moon Age Day 23   Moon Sign Capricorn*

am . . . .

pm . . . .
Not only could you presently be feeling a good deal less assertive than
was the case yesterday, your general sensitivity is going right off the scale.
The spiritual heart of Aries is diametrically opposed to the go-getter you
sometimes have to be. Why not use today to explore the deep, inner
quality that you so rarely address?

3 SUNDAY ☿ *Moon Age Day 24   Moon Sign Aquarius*

am . . . .

pm . . . .
Your co-operative spirit is potentially strong, a fact that isn't lost on
others, many of whom are quite happy to pitch in with you. There is a
distinct possibility that you can come to terms with someone who had
openly hated you in the past. Getting rid of an enemy may prove far more
important than you presently appreciate.

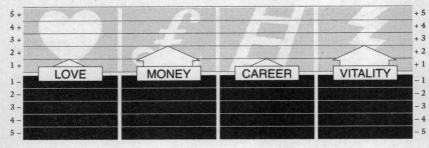

April 2005

YOUR MONTH AT A GLANCE

⊕ = Opportunities are around   ⊖ = Be on the defensive   ⬤ = Life is pretty ordinary

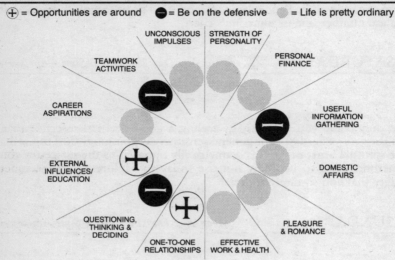

UNCONSCIOUS IMPULSES

STRENGTH OF PERSONALITY

TEAMWORK ACTIVITIES

PERSONAL FINANCE

CAREER ASPIRATIONS

USEFUL INFORMATION GATHERING

EXTERNAL INFLUENCES/ EDUCATION

DOMESTIC AFFAIRS

QUESTIONING, THINKING & DECIDING

ONE-TO-ONE RELATIONSHIPS

EFFECTIVE WORK & HEALTH

PLEASURE & ROMANCE

APRIL HIGHS AND LOWS

Here I show you how the rhythms of the Moon will affect you this month. Like the tide, your energies and abilities will rise and fall with its pattern. When it is above the centre line, go for it, when it is below, you should be resting.

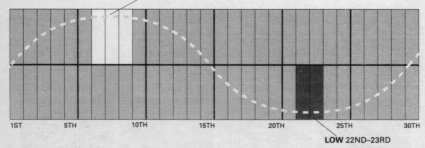

HIGH 7TH–9TH

1ST   5TH   10TH   15TH   20TH   25TH   30TH

LOW 22ND–23RD

70

4 MONDAY ☿ Moon Age Day 25 Moon Sign Aquarius

am . . . .

pm . . . .
When it comes to major initiatives you needn't hold back. This is one of those days when Aries can show its real mettle and insist on getting its own way at every turn. As long as you remember to bear in mind that other people have opinions too, you should be able to get away with forcing your ideas through.

5 TUESDAY ☿ Moon Age Day 26 Moon Sign Pisces

am . . . .

pm . . . .
As a direct contrast to yesterday, it is possible you will prefer your own company for the moment. Some Aries people will be in the middle of a keep-fit campaign, so you may be jogging in the park or going to the gym. As important as it is to look after your physical health, you also need some meditation now.

6 WEDNESDAY ☿ Moon Age Day 27 Moon Sign Pisces

am . . . .

pm . . . .
Getting along with others today may not be the easiest of tasks. It is possible that those around you seem to be doing everything they can to throw a spanner in the works. Of course, this is just the way you see things at the moment and you should be wise enough to realise the fact. If you don't, trouble could follow.

7 THURSDAY ☿ Moon Age Day 28 Moon Sign Aries

am . . . .

pm . . . .
The green light is on and it seems certain that you intend to push forward as hard and as fast as you can. With little to stand in your way, it is professional matters that show strongest in the glare of the lunar high this month. Don't take no for an answer and be willing to go that extra step if necessary.

8 FRIDAY ☿ *Moon Age Day 0   Moon Sign Aries*

am . . . .

pm . . . .
All your dreams and schemes come together at this time, simply waiting
from the right sort of initiatives from you in order to become reality. You
could be bowled over by the very positive reactions you get from others,
leaving you feeling that forward progress is going to be even easier.

9 SATURDAY ☿ *Moon Age Day 1   Moon Sign Aries*

am . . . .

pm . . . .
It's a three-day lunar high this time around, extending into the weekend.
That enables you to give your social life a definite boost. The only slight
fly in the ointment is that you may be trying too hard, which could so
easily lead to a degree of exhaustion by Sunday. Slow and steady wins the
race under present trends.

10 SUNDAY ☿ *Moon Age Day 2   Moon Sign Taurus*

am . . . .

pm . . . .
When it comes to being number one in the social diaries of everyone else,
you should have little trouble at present. Make life easy for yourself by
showing the real charm of which you are capable. With the year
advancing and slightly warmer days on the cards, you should be getting
out and about more, perhaps with friends this Sunday.

	LOVE	MONEY	CAREER	VITALITY

11 MONDAY   ☿   *Moon Age Day 3   Moon Sign Taurus*

am . . . .

pm . . . .
Certain financial decisions are made this month from a position of
security. Even if you don't find it especially easy to convince at least one
person that you know what you are talking about, it is worth that extra
bit of effort to have a go. The attitude of friends generally can be rather
confusing at present.

12 TUESDAY   *Moon Age Day 4   Moon Sign Gemini*

am . . . .

pm . . . .
Get out and about as much as possible today. You don't need to tell
everyone your business, and indeed it might be a mistake to do so.
Continue past efforts to get ahead in the financial stakes and do be
prepared to count every penny right now because you are likely to need
more cash before very long.

13 WEDNESDAY   *Moon Age Day 5   Moon Sign Gemini*

am . . . .

pm . . . .
A more competitive edge is noticeable for Aries now. Even during the
lunar high you were not quite as finely tuned as you can be when it comes
to making those very important decisions. Keeping a note of the attitude
of friends and relatives would be no bad thing. They may be behaving
somewhat oddly right now.

14 THURSDAY   *Moon Age Day 6   Moon Sign Cancer*

am . . . .

pm . . . .
If you seem to be at loggerheads in a friendship, it really would be
sensible to stand back and look at things in a different way, rather than
slogging it out with someone you like very much. To retreat from such a
situation is not a sign of defeat, but rather a mark of your intelligence.

15 FRIDAY
Moon Age Day 7   Moon Sign Cancer

am . . . .

pm . . . .
There may be high spots in the money-making department. If you have been sensible of late, you will have just a little cash to spare and can use it to invest wisely. Rash decisions ought to be avoided. Meanwhile, you can make the most of romantic opportunities, for some of you from unexpected directions.

16 SATURDAY
Moon Age Day 8   Moon Sign Cancer

am . . . .

pm . . . .
An issue from the past is inclined to raise its head again, much to your disapproval. Treat such situations with great circumspection and don't allow yourself to be too quick to react. Patience is a virtue, though all too often it is one you don't possess in great measure. Confidence might seem lacking, but it is there if you look.

17 SUNDAY
Moon Age Day 9   Moon Sign Leo

am . . . .

pm . . . .
When it comes to love and romance, you could hardly find a better time than this one has potential to be. It appears you are now willing to drop some of the responsibility and you will show on the way that you have time for the people who are really important in your life. It is important not to allow yourself to become tense.

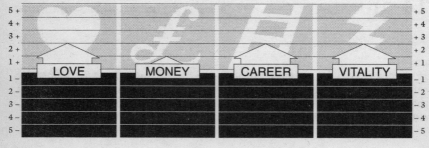

18 MONDAY   *Moon Age Day 10   Moon Sign Leo*

am . . . .

pm . . . .
Compromises may be easy at home, or in personal attachments, though much more difficult at work. There is a great difference between the various sides of your nature right now and this is a situation you really do have to address. You would be wise to complete one job before you get started on another.

19 TUESDAY   *Moon Age Day 11   Moon Sign Virgo*

am . . . .

pm . . . .
Trends suggest that your sense of determination isn't in doubt, merely the methods you are using to prove your ideas are sound. You need to listen to what others are saying and genuinely take their opinions on board. You can be a good team player but that doesn't always mean being in total charge of the team!

20 WEDNESDAY   *Moon Age Day 12   Moon Sign Virgo*

am . . . .

pm . . . .
Financially and in terms of work, there are now matters that you can simply sit back and allow to mature in their own good time. This allows you moments to look around. Since you may now be in a contemplative frame of mind, this is going to prove a rewarding period. All Aries people need to think from time to time.

21 THURSDAY   *Moon Age Day 13   Moon Sign Virgo*

am . . . .

pm . . . .
Even if you still enjoy being on the go, there could be a part of your nature that wants to sit by a gently flowing stream or walk on a deserted beach. The time of year might mitigate against this, but you can get just as much out of watching a movie or reading a good book. All work is not the answer today.

22 FRIDAY
Moon Age Day 14   Moon Sign Libra

am . . . .

pm . . . .
Despite the arrival of the lunar low, you have scope to thrust yourself into the very centre of whatever action is taking place in your vicinity. Conforming to expectations may not be easy because you so often think others don't know what they are talking about. Balance is hard to find, but vital.

23 SATURDAY
Moon Age Day 15   Moon Sign Libra

am . . . .

pm . . . .
It would probably be best to let others make some of the decisions today. The lunar low could be sapping your strength somewhat and making it difficult for you to see the wood for the trees. Just about the only aspect of life that this doesn't affect is romance. This is exactly the right day to be whispering words of love.

24 SUNDAY
Moon Age Day 16   Moon Sign Scorpio

am . . . .

pm . . . .
Even if your confidence still isn't exactly high, if you are willing to listen to your relatives and friends, this shouldn't really matter. When it comes to getting things done, it is possible that you will constantly be broken off today. That's simply part of the astrological package on offer and there is little or nothing to be done about it.

25 MONDAY
Moon Age Day 17   Moon Sign Scorpio

am . . . .

pm . . . .
With the lunar low well out of the way you are able to work and play with equal determination. Although it might not always seem to be the case, things are probably going very well for you at present. Just a few minutes spend realising that fact would make you calmer and more willing to wait for the prizes.

26 TUESDAY
Moon Age Day 18   Moon Sign Sagittarius

am . . . .

pm . . . .
Watch out for financial fluctuations, which might take you more or less by surprise. Your creative potential is good, though may not extend to money matters. In a family sense, you are probably wise enough to let someone else make the running, at least for the next couple of days and maybe even longer.

27 WEDNESDAY
Moon Age Day 19   Moon Sign Sagittarius

am . . . .

pm . . . .
It feels as though personal freedom is the key to contentment and indeed, up to a point, this is true. However, there are other issues that need to be addressed, not least if your partner is behaving rather oddly. Instead of simply wondering what it going on, it might be sensible to ask a few leading questions.

28 THURSDAY
Moon Age Day 20   Moon Sign Capricorn

am . . . .

pm . . . .
Now you are entering a period when you have what it takes to bring certain career matters to a head. This is a time during which some Aries people will be taking on new jobs, or consolidating existing responsibilities. Whatever you decide to do, stay cool, calm and collected and don't betray your excitement.

29 FRIDAY
Moon Age Day 21   Moon Sign Capricorn

am . . . .

pm . . . .
Aries is on a roll. All the practical skills at your disposal are showing themselves clearly as April draws to an end. This is probably just as well, particularly if there are many demands being made of you. Splitting your responsibilities could be sensible, and even sharing a few of them with other people if you find it possible.

30 SATURDAY
Moon Age Day 22   Moon Sign Aquarius

am . . . .

pm . . . .
You need a degree of courage today in order to refuse the requests of people who may be in a more elevated position than you are. Guts are something all Aries people possess, even if you doubt the fact yourself. There are moments today when you simply want to be at home and in the midst of those who love you.

1 SUNDAY
Moon Age Day 23   Moon Sign Aquarius

am . . . .

pm . . . .
Although your social life might seem somewhat less impressive today than you would wish, the situation generally is within your own hands. Don't be too quick to judge others, especially in personal matters. Why not simply go with the flow and allow yourself to laugh at the foolishness you observe out there in the wider world?

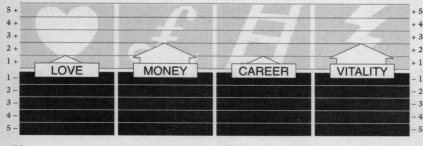

May 2005

YOUR MONTH AT A GLANCE

⊕ = Opportunities are around   ⊖ = Be on the defensive   ● = Life is pretty ordinary

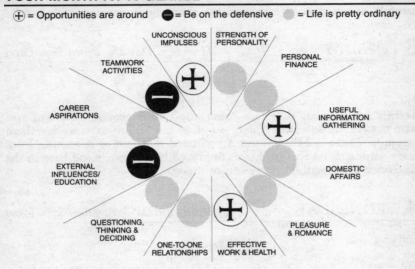

MAY HIGHS AND LOWS

Here I show you how the rhythms of the Moon will affect you this month. Like the tide, your energies and abilities will rise and fall with its pattern. When it is above the centre line, go for it, when it is below, you should be resting.

HIGH 5TH–6TH

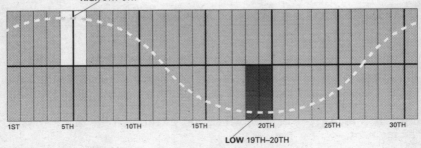

LOW 19TH–20TH

2 MONDAY
Moon Age Day 24   Moon Sign Aquarius

am ....

pm ....
Personal money matters should continue to go through a generally settled phase, leaving you with the time to think about other things. Before you do, it is worth considering that investments laid down carefully at this time have potential to show significant dividends later.

3 TUESDAY
Moon Age Day 25   Moon Sign Pisces

am ....

pm ....
Trends suggest that there are some good ideas around now and you won't want to squander them, so it is important to consider them carefully. There is help around if you need it, some of it coming from fairly surprising directions. Love could well be on your mind later in the day, once the practicalities are out of the way.

4 WEDNESDAY
Moon Age Day 26   Moon Sign Pisces

am ....

pm ....
Even if there is slightly less in the way of rewards coming from one or two friendships, there are still people around who prove to be reliable. Concern for family members is probably understandable, though possibly not quite as necessary as it appears. Beware of being too quick to jump to any conclusion at the moment.

5 THURSDAY
Moon Age Day 27   Moon Sign Aries

am ....

pm ....
As the Moon moves into your sign, so you find the vitality you need to put the finishing touches to tasks that have been outstanding for some time now. You should find yourself well able to relax and yet get masses done. It is the sheer ease with which you go through life that counts at the moment.

6 FRIDAY

Moon Age Day 28   Moon Sign Aries

am ....

pm ....

You have a particularly persuasive tongue at present, so bringing others round to your point of view should be within your power. No one person is better than any other when it comes to getting the assistance you need with a new project, if only because you have the ability to enlist whatever support you need.

7 SATURDAY

Moon Age Day 29   Moon Sign Taurus

am ....

pm ....

There may be some undue pressure put upon you, most likely in a career sense. This should be like water off a duck's back, as long as you don't get into a reactive frame of mind. Realise that everyone has their own song to sing, which is fine as long as you merely go on humming your own too.

8 SUNDAY

Moon Age Day 0   Moon Sign Taurus

am ....

pm ....

A new and positive phase affecting property and finance is on the cards. For this you can thank Venus in your solar second house. Things flow much better for the next few days and it takes less effort on your part to convince the world that you know what you are talking about and what action others should take.

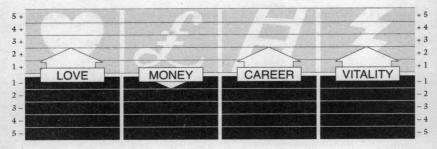

9 MONDAY   *Moon Age Day 1   Moon Sign Gemini*

am . . . .

pm . . . .
A variety of interests should prove rewarding today and you are much less likely to be nervy or somehow on edge. Aries tends to get a little ragged in a mental sense when it is necessary to concentrate on one fact exclusively. Conforming to social expectations could be something of a chore, but is probably necessary.

10 TUESDAY   *Moon Age Day 2   Moon Sign Gemini*

am . . . .

pm . . . .
Now you have scope to ensure that the pace of life becomes swift but pleasant. Try to make good use of information that comes your way. The more unlikely the direction, the greater is the chance that what you are hearing makes sense. The odd, the unusual and the downright barmy all have a part to play in your unique thinking at the moment.

11 WEDNESDAY   *Moon Age Day 3   Moon Sign Gemini*

am . . . .

pm . . . .
This is a time during which your general popularity could hit an all-time high. Venus is in an extremely good position now as far as you are concerned, enabling you to make sure others look again at the unique quality of your nature. This can be a help professionally but is more pronounced at a social and even a personal level.

12 THURSDAY   *Moon Age Day 4   Moon Sign Cancer*

am . . . .

pm . . . .
There are signs that a good percentage of your time today is taken up thinking about practical matters and especially money. Beware of pushing yourself harder than is necessary, though, because social trends are also good and it might be pleasant to spend at least a few hours today simply finding ways to enjoy yourself.

13 FRIDAY
Moon Age Day 5   Moon Sign Cancer

am . . . .

pm . . . .
It's Friday the thirteenth, though that shouldn't have much of a bearing on your day since the majority of Aries people refuse to set any store by such things. Surprise, surprise then, when one or two of your little schemes begin to go pear-shaped. Of course this is a coincidence, but it might make you think.

14 SATURDAY
Moon Age Day 6   Moon Sign Leo

am . . . .

pm . . . .
There is a slight accent on the negative now, even if this is not coming specifically from your direction. You may see fewer opportunities on the horizon, a state of affairs that won't please you too much. One thing is certain: arguing for your limitations is going to make them much more obvious to everyone.

15 SUNDAY
Moon Age Day 7   Moon Sign Leo

am . . . .

pm . . . .
Along comes a good time to put yourself about socially. Some of the slightly negative trends of the last couple of days recede into the distance, leaving you feeling that you would be interested in more friendship contacts. There is someone, or even a group of people, who would probably welcome your company.

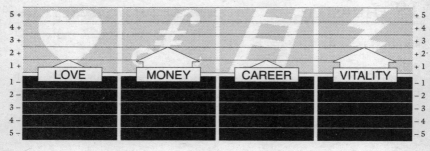

16 MONDAY
Moon Age Day 8   Moon Sign Leo

am . . . .

pm . . . .
A calmer and even a more contemplative Aries is now on display. The
depth of your thinking is potentially much greater than would normally
be the case and you may even surprise yourself with your sensitivity. It's
almost as if you can 'feel' the way other people are thinking, and you can
predict their likely actions and responses.

17 TUESDAY
Moon Age Day 9   Moon Sign Virgo

am . . . .

pm . . . .
It's time to put some of your clever ideas to the test, though you would
be wise to be certain about specifics before you risk too much time or any
money. Why not seek out the advice of someone who clearly knows what
they are talking about and enlist their support? Routines can be quite
tedious today, so stay away from them if possible.

18 WEDNESDAY
Moon Age Day 10   Moon Sign Virgo

am . . . .

pm . . . .
It is possible that a friend could see more clearly than you just how useful
a specific investment in terms of money or time could prove to be. If
their insights are definitely stronger now, it would be well worthwhile to
offer them an ear. Confronting opponents is not something you should
do today.

19 THURSDAY
Moon Age Day 11   Moon Sign Libra

am . . . .

pm . . . .
You would be wise to slow down the pace of progress, even deliberately,
while the lunar low is around. The problem it brings is that no matter
how much effort you choose to put into projects, you will make little
headway. Better by far to stand on the bank of the river of life and watch
the water flow. The experience can be very rewarding.

20 FRIDAY
Moon Age Day 12   Moon Sign Libra

am . . . .

pm . . . .
Another day on which you could well discover that getting ahead is far less easy than would normally be the case. However, today is especially good for planning ahead and for talking to friends and family members alike. Concern for the underdog may also be evident – not a usual trait for Aries.

21 SATURDAY
Moon Age Day 13   Moon Sign Scorpio

am . . . .

pm . . . .
Much swifter progress can be achieved today, though probably not in a career sense unless you are a weekend worker. Decisions you recently took can now be made to take shape, especially if they concern your medium-term future. Social trends are emphasised, so you might choose to embark on an enjoyable weekend.

22 SUNDAY
Moon Age Day 14   Moon Sign Scorpio

am . . . .

pm . . . .
Communication issues are highlighted today, for both positive and negative reasons. Certainly your curiosity is aroused very easily and you may even decide to chase a rainbow or two. This is not a day on which to confront others or during which you should take yourself at all seriously.

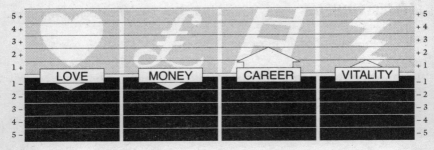

23 MONDAY
Moon Age Day 15   Moon Sign Scorpio

am . . . .

pm . . . .
There seem to be helpful influences available where money situations are
concerned, though it is possible that you will have to look carefully for
them since they are unlikely to seek you out. Thinking deeply at the
moment, you may decide that a change of strategy is necessary,
particularly with regard to personal attachments.

24 TUESDAY
Moon Age Day 16   Moon Sign Sagittarius

am . . . .

pm . . . .
Emotional matters could well preoccupy you now, which is why you need
other matters on which to concentrate from time to time. Don't worry
too much about the way those around you are behaving. Just as surely as
your astrological fortunes fluctuate, so do theirs. A day to keep an open
mind about inevitable changes at home.

25 WEDNESDAY
Moon Age Day 17   Moon Sign Sagittarius

am . . . .

pm . . . .
You now have more scope for social niceties and for doing the 'expected'
thing. Although the weekend is still a few days away, it is likely that you
are already thinking about the potentials it offers. This is an ideal time to
enjoy what is going on intellectually and even culturally in your
immediate surroundings.

26 THURSDAY
Moon Age Day 18   Moon Sign Capricorn

am . . . .

pm . . . .
If you enjoy being in the social mainstream at the moment, you will
probably not be concentrating quite as much on practical matters as has
been the case earlier in the month. With the weather improving and
spring showing itself around every corner, it becomes more important to
you to get out and about.

27 FRIDAY
Moon Age Day 19   Moon Sign Capricorn

am . . . .

pm . . . .
You have what it takes to get practical matters to go your way, even
without you having to try very hard. It isn't that life generally is a picnic
at the moment, but you do show a distinctly contemplative side to your
nature and will find others easy to get along with. There are powerful and
useful trends building in your life.

28 SATURDAY
Moon Age Day 20   Moon Sign Aquarius

am . . . .

pm . . . .
A useful boost to communication skills make it possible for you to take
the plans you have laid down for the weekend and to use them positively.
Frustration should be kept to a minimum, though it is worth mentioning
that there may be family members who simply refuse to conform to your
expectations of them.

29 SUNDAY
Moon Age Day 21   Moon Sign Aquarius

am . . . .

pm . . . .
Now is the time to relax into whatever you are doing and enjoy what life
is naturally offering. You might decide that something different is
necessary, and with the Moon presently in Aquarius it might even be a
mildly eccentric sort of adventure. Giving yourself time to rest would be
no bad thing, even if you do so in a dynamic way.

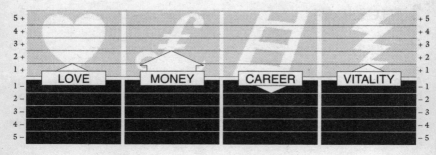

30 MONDAY

Moon Age Day 22   Moon Sign Pisces

am ....

pm ....
It is not a good idea to believe everything you hear today. Although it is
unlikely that anyone is deliberately trying to pull the wool over your eyes,
you may be more easily fooled at the moment than would generally be
the case. A day to protect your interests in some way, even if you have to
go to some trouble to do so.

31 TUESDAY

Moon Age Day 23   Moon Sign Pisces

am ....

pm ....
Your usually desire for personal freedom should be easy to satisfy at the
moment. There might not be quite the opportunities you had hoped to
get ahead financially at this time, though there are many more ways to
please yourself through money. Relationships offer significant
rewards under present trends.

1 WEDNESDAY

Moon Age Day 24   Moon Sign Aries

am ....

pm ....
As the lunar low arrives you can ensure that major undertakings go as
planned, but you might have to modify your approach on more than one
occasion today. Remain flexible and invent your universe as you go along.
The more you show the variable qualities within your nature, the greater
is the attention you can get from others.

2 THURSDAY

Moon Age Day 25   Moon Sign Aries

am ....

pm ....
A few slightly odd astrological trends tended to cloud the first day of the
lunar high for you, but today is very different. Now you should have
everything in place to launch a major coup of some sort. Planetary
interaction being what it is for you at the moment, it might be your
career that becomes the main focus of your attention.

3 FRIDAY

Moon Age Day 26   Moon Sign Taurus

am . . . .

pm . . . .
This is a very interesting day to be in the thick of things. Mercury is now in your solar third house, which has to be especially good with regard to communication. Getting what you want from others should be a piece of cake, though of what sort totally depends on the way you go about bringing them round.

4 SATURDAY

Moon Age Day 27   Moon Sign Taurus

am . . . .

pm . . . .
You have scope to make positive things happen in and around your home at this time. It would be good to start Saturday early because if you remain in bed too long you will find restrictions developing later. Someone you haven't seen for a long time could well return to your life in the very near future.

5 SUNDAY

Moon Age Day 28   Moon Sign Taurus

am . . . .

pm . . . .
A less than dynamic Aries is now on display, thanks to the present position of Mars in your solar twelfth house. You could feel as if some of your potential is being wasted, though in reality all that most of your plans need to continue is attention and more time. Instead of fretting, why not find ways in which to enjoy the day?

June 2005

YOUR MONTH AT A GLANCE

⊕ = Opportunities are around　⊖ = Be on the defensive　⬤ = Life is pretty ordinary

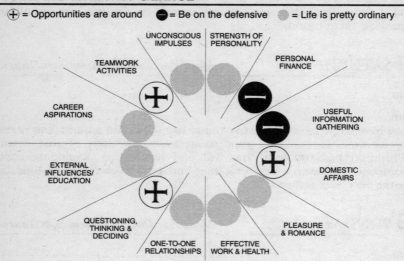

JUNE HIGHS AND LOWS

Here I show you how the rhythms of the Moon will affect you this month. Like the tide, your energies and abilities will rise and fall with its pattern. When it is above the centre line, go for it, when it is below, you should be resting.

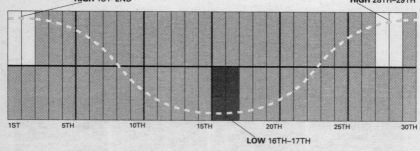

6 MONDAY

Moon Age Day 0   Moon Sign Gemini

am . . . .

pm . . . .
Right now, travel and cultural matters should be high on your personal agenda. It appears that the more refined qualities of your nature are to the fore, and you will want to demonstrate them to the world. If there are a mountain of jobs to be done, your best response is to deal with them one at a time and steadily.

7 TUESDAY

Moon Age Day 1   Moon Sign Gemini

am . . . .

pm . . . .
The influence of the Moon in your solar third house could enable you to free yourself from certain commitments you haven't been relishing at all. With a greater sense of freedom today, you have scope to seek out new ways to pep up your social life. Keeping hold of money might be difficult, but it isn't impossible.

8 WEDNESDAY

Moon Age Day 2   Moon Sign Cancer

am . . . .

pm . . . .
Beware of allowing domestic obligations to get in the way of matters that are likely to be more enjoyable and possibly also rewarding. It might seem at times as though you have nothing particularly interesting to say, though those around you would be surprised at this, because they find you fascinating.

9 THURSDAY

Moon Age Day 3   Moon Sign Cancer

am . . . .

pm . . . .
Now is the time to keep your eyes and ears open for any new information coming to you from the big world outside. Even the smallest pieces of information can be used to bolster your own ideas, and there are some important lessons to be learned. Romance is high on your agenda for today, even if you don't realise the fact.

10 FRIDAY

Moon Age Day 4   Moon Sign Cancer

am ....

pm ....
Even if you decide to retreat from the world today, there is a good chance it will find ways and means to follow you. Mars is in your solar twelfth house, so it is possible that you don't have quite the verve and dynamism that would normally be the case. However, you are an Aries subject, and that shows.

11 SATURDAY

Moon Age Day 5   Moon Sign Leo

am ....

pm ....
Romantic involvements may not be offering quite the potential they did a couple of days ago. The fault is not yours, but comes from a combination of astrological trends, few of which are favouring this aspect of life. On a practical front things should be better and you might choose today to seek advancement.

12 SUNDAY

Moon Age Day 6   Moon Sign Leo

am ....

pm ....
You need to keep life as interesting and varied as you can. You can become bored very easily because you feel lazy but at the same time experience frustration if you are not getting ahead as you would wish. Simply show a little patience, because circumstances are likely to change before very long.

13 MONDAY   *Moon Age Day 7   Moon Sign Virgo*

am ....

pm ....
Mars is now entering your solar first house, allowing you to dispel some
of the frustration that has become obvious during the last few days. Now
you have more opportunities and a greater amount of energy to put into
projects you simply know are going to work out to your advantage.
Don't worry too much about the way others see you.

14 TUESDAY   *Moon Age Day 8   Moon Sign Virgo*

am ....

pm ....
Avoid getting obsessed about anything, particularly a work issue that you
cannot alter. If you are willing to go with the flow and to co-operate with
people you instinctively trust, matters are apt to sort themselves out. This
leaves you somewhat freer to get on with patching up a dent in an
important relationship.

15 WEDNESDAY   *Moon Age Day 9   Moon Sign Virgo*

am ....

pm ....
Personal freedom is important today and you can so easily feel fettered
by circumstances. Find some way to prove to yourself that you are in
charge of your own life and move away from situations that tie your
hands for weeks or months to come. You can afford to give yourself some
free time simply to do what pleases you.

16 THURSDAY   *Moon Age Day 10   Moon Sign Libra*

am ....

pm ....
It would not be a bad thing to slow down today. In reality, you may have
very little choice. The lunar low could inhibit you from making the
general progress you might wish, and as long as you don't go knocking
your head against a brick wall needlessly, today could prove to be
rewarding in low-key ways.

17 FRIDAY

Moon Age Day 11   Moon Sign Libra

am . . . .

pm . . . .
Keeping to tried and tested paths works best for you at the moment.
There isn't much to be gained from chancing your arm, especially in
monetary terms. There is still enjoyment to be had, though it may not be
of the exciting sort. Family members might be pleased to see more of
you, as might certain friends.

18 SATURDAY

Moon Age Day 12   Moon Sign Scorpio

am . . . .

pm . . . .
Harmonious personal encounters could well pep up the weekend, and
the potential excitement they bring blows away the fog of the lunar low
period. Now you should be feeling more like your old self, even if there
are one or two people around who seem determined to throw some sort
of spanner in the works.

19 SUNDAY

Moon Age Day 13   Moon Sign Scorpio

am . . . .

pm . . . .
The signs are that you are back in a generally competitive frame of mind
and able to take the world on. What might prove somewhat frustrating
on this Sunday is the realisation that nobody wants to confront you! All
is peace and harmony in your vicinity and it would certainly be a shame
to change that, simply because you are restless.

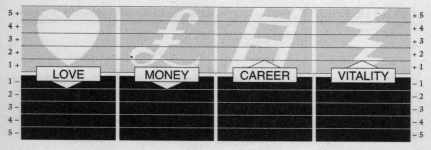

20 MONDAY   *Moon Age Day 14   Moon Sign Sagittarius*

am . . . .

pm . . . .
Social and travel matters can keep you busy in equal proportions at the
start of this working week. What will probably seem less interesting are
the responsibilities of your everyday life. There is a tendency to shift your
problems onto the shoulders of others, which probably isn't the best way
to proceed.

21 TUESDAY   *Moon Age Day 15   Moon Sign Sagittarius*

am . . . .

pm . . . .
Trends indicate that there may be some reason to celebrate today, which
you will do with great willingness. A change of scene or a social get-
together really suits you right now. Some Aries subjects may even be
considering taking a holiday at this time. If so, you could hardly have
chosen more wisely, because trends are good.

22 WEDNESDAY   *Moon Age Day 16   Moon Sign Capricorn*

am . . . .

pm . . . .
The more positive face of Aries begins to show itself, which is why you
could be accused of throwing your weight around today. This is not a
situation you should relish, because it can lose you some allies at an
important stage in your life. A lower-key and more humble attitude is
more likely to pay dividends now.

23 THURSDAY   *Moon Age Day 17   Moon Sign Capricorn*

am . . . .

pm . . . .
This is likely to be a 'business as usual' sort of day. It doesn't lack
potential, but neither are you likely to find yourself pushing over any
buses. You have to realise that you cannot be pushing forward at full
speed all the time. Contemplative days such as this have a greater
importance than you sometimes realise.

24 FRIDAY

Moon Age Day 18   Moon Sign Aquarius

am . . . .

pm . . . .
You can do just about anything today – with a little help from your friends. This is not a go-it-alone sort of period. If you refuse to accept this fact you could be in for a roller-coaster ride and have to take all the consequences of your actions. Sharing is better, especially as things can go slightly wrong.

25 SATURDAY

Moon Age Day 19   Moon Sign Aquarius

am . . . .

pm . . . .
Beware of relying entirely on your intuition today, even if it seems to be working strongly. You can still be fooled and may discover that a few people in your vicinity are not at all what you thought them to be. You also need to be aware that situations can change very quickly, which is a certain fact at the moment.

26 SUNDAY

Moon Age Day 20   Moon Sign Pisces

am . . . .

pm . . . .
The domestic atmosphere at home is definitely boosted by the presence of the Sun in your solar fourth house. For the next month or so you can ensure that your relationships with family members not only improve but are much more important than would usually be the case. There are signs that someone needs your advice.

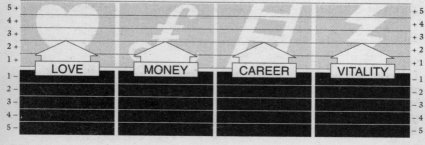

27 MONDAY   *Moon Age Day 21   Moon Sign Pisces*

am . . . .

pm . . . .
You have what it takes to make this a particularly rewarding time, especially at home. There is a certain quietness in your life ahead of the lunar high, but this merely offers you the time you need to plan carefully. A more contemplative Aries subject looks out at the world, a factor that certainly is not lost on your nearest and dearest.

28 TUESDAY   *Moon Age Day 22   Moon Sign Aries*

am . . . .

pm . . . .
This is potentially the most progressive and rewarding part of the month. It could seem as though all your energy has returned on the same day and it is highly unlikely that anything will hold you back for long. Countering the slightly negative remarks and attitudes of specific friends ought to be quite easy at this time.

29 WEDNESDAY   *Moon Age Day 23   Moon Sign Aries*

am . . . .

pm . . . .
A day to make an early start and get as much done as you can. Influences today are favourable professionally and in almost every other way. Keeping abreast of what is happening in your world should be easy and you also have the additional reward of knowing that others are working hard on your behalf.

30 THURSDAY   *Moon Age Day 24   Moon Sign Taurus*

am . . . .

pm . . . .
A high-energy period when your powers are at their peak. Mars is in your solar first house, offering the sort of energy that Aries relishes. Don't be too quick to forge ahead with plans until you have the permission and probably the advice of someone who clearly knows better than you what they are talking about.

1 FRIDAY

Moon Age Day 25   Moon Sign Taurus

am . . . .

pm . . . .
Stand by for a fairly hectic phase and one during which you might have little or no time for the niceties of life. People should forgive you for being slightly offhand, particularly if at least some of your efforts are geared in their direction. Concentrating on anything to do with family or friendship may be virtually impossible.

2 SATURDAY

Moon Age Day 26   Moon Sign Taurus

am . . . .

pm . . . .
There is a tendency for you to be restless right now and that means filling your weekend with interesting diversions. Chances are that you are well up with the practical aspects of life and you can probably afford to give some time to yourself. You would be wise to keep away from get-rich-quick schemes, which probably won't work.

3 SUNDAY

Moon Age Day 27   Moon Sign Gemini

am . . . .

pm . . . .
When it comes to expressing yourself today, you should be second to none. Conforming to expectations may not be easy, but then it is the originality within your nature that appeals so much to others at present. You can get an audience, no matter what you choose to do. What is more, you relish being in the limelight.

July 2005

YOUR MONTH AT A GLANCE

⊕ = Opportunities are around   ⊖ = Be on the defensive   ◯ = Life is pretty ordinary

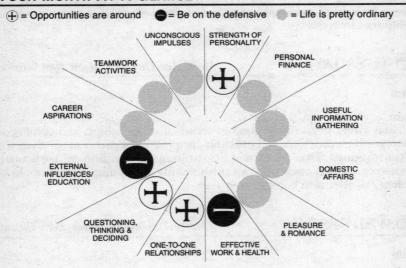

UNCONSCIOUS IMPULSES

STRENGTH OF PERSONALITY

TEAMWORK ACTIVITIES

PERSONAL FINANCE ⊕

CAREER ASPIRATIONS

USEFUL INFORMATION GATHERING

EXTERNAL INFLUENCES/ EDUCATION ⊖

DOMESTIC AFFAIRS

⊕ QUESTIONING, THINKING & DECIDING

⊕ ONE-TO-ONE RELATIONSHIPS

⊖ EFFECTIVE WORK & HEALTH

PLEASURE & ROMANCE

JULY HIGHS AND LOWS

Here I show you how the rhythms of the Moon will affect you this month. Like the tide, your energies and abilities will rise and fall with its pattern. When it is above the centre line, go for it, when it is below, you should be resting.

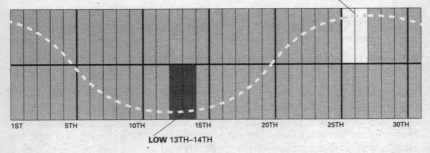

HIGH 26TH–27TH

1ST   5TH   10TH   15TH   20TH   25TH   30TH

LOW 13TH–14TH

99

4 MONDAY

Moon Age Day 28   Moon Sign Gemini

am . . . .

pm . . . .
Right now you should be on the lookout for newcomers on the social scene. There are gains to be made financially, even if these prove to be of a fairly small nature. With a certain restlessness in your nature today it is very important that you are able to spread yourself across a range of different interests.

5 TUESDAY

Moon Age Day 29   Moon Sign Gemini

am . . . .

pm . . . .
Today could prove fairly good in terms of relationships, and coming to terms with a colleague will probably turn out to be rather easier than you had imagined. Don't be too quick to jump to conclusions, particularly with regard to the way your lover is thinking and acting. There should be plenty of attention coming your way.

6 WEDNESDAY

Moon Age Day 0   Moon Sign Cancer

am . . . .

pm . . . .
Favourable domestic relationships make it easier for you to concentrate on practical matters, without spending too much time sorting out the problems of your family. You needn't be stuck for something to do socially, but there are times today when you could quite easily get bored with the same old routines.

7 THURSDAY

Moon Age Day 1   Moon Sign Cancer

am . . . .

pm . . . .
Romance remains positively highlighted, making this potentially one of the best weeks of the year so far in personal terms. You can be particularly charming and show those you love just how important they are to you. Holding on to cash for the moment would be no bad thing, because the ideal time for speculation hasn't quite arrived.

8 FRIDAY
Moon Age Day 2   Moon Sign Cancer

am . . . .

pm . . . .
With more pressure noticeable at home, it is possible that younger family members give you some cause for concern. The attitude of friends could also be somewhat puzzling, which might mean having to ask some leading questions at some stage today. Keep abreast of events out there in the big, wide world.

9 SATURDAY
Moon Age Day 3   Moon Sign Leo

am . . . .

pm . . . .
Love life and social issues enable you to make this an interesting and even exciting weekend. Although you might not get as much done as you would have wished, you can always catch up with jobs later. For now, go out and have a good time, probably in the company of your lover or relatives, rather than with friends.

10 SUNDAY
Moon Age Day 4   Moon Sign Leo

am . . . .

pm . . . .
Success is possible today if you are properly organised. Leaving situations to chance won't work half as well as preparing yourself for eventualities in advance and there is plenty of help around if you are willing to ask the right questions. Conforming to expectations could prove somewhat difficult later in the day.

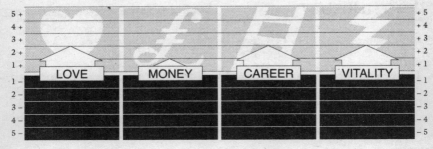

11 MONDAY
Moon Age Day 5   Moon Sign Virgo

am . . . .

pm . . . .
This is a time during which you have what it takes to be the centre of attention. Venus is presently in your solar fifth house. As a result, you have everything you need to attract people to you like iron filings to a magnet. Older people could have some very special advice to offer, and it is well worth listening.

12 TUESDAY
Moon Age Day 6   Moon Sign Virgo

am . . . .

pm . . . .
It is possible that you will come across to others more forcefully than you intend at the moment. At the same time, you have scope to be creative and to show a distinct flair when it comes to your looks and general attitude. This proves to be the right combination of attributes to get ahead at work and even to advance further than you expected.

13 WEDNESDAY
Moon Age Day 7   Moon Sign Libra

am . . . .

pm . . . .
As a direct contradiction to yesterday, today shows that others are getting ahead better than you are, and this can be a cause of frustration. Avoid arguments and be especially careful to stay away from those sour grapes. If you appear rational, cool and collected, you can still get your own way in the end.

14 THURSDAY
Moon Age Day 8   Moon Sign Libra

am . . . .

pm . . . .
The reason there is a continuing downturn in situations can be summed in two words, 'lunar low'. This is that time during which the Moon occupies the zodiac sign opposite to your own. You might simply have to settle for second best today, knowing that by tomorrow trends will be looking more progressive again.

15 FRIDAY   *Moon Age Day 9   Moon Sign Scorpio*

am . . . .

pm . . . .
You can now put recent delays aside and exploit a tendency towards innovative thinking that really stands you in good stead. At the same time, you should be noticeably relaxed on the outside, even if you are shaking like a leaf in your mind. Avoid putting yourself through more pressure than turns out to be necessary.

16 SATURDAY   *Moon Age Day 10   Moon Sign Scorpio*

am . . . .

pm . . . .
There should be enough happening in your personal and domestic scene to keep you happy and fulfilled during the weekend. Although the things others want you to do will sometimes go against the grain, in the main you are likely to enjoy the cut and thrust of a busy and eventful social life. Family members can be quite precious.

17 SUNDAY   *Moon Age Day 11   Moon Sign Sagittarius*

am . . . .

pm . . . .
This might be an excellent time for a genuine and far-reaching change of scene. With the summer weather around, and knowing that you have bought yourself some time, you would be well advised to head for a high mountain or a very blue sea. If the pressure of work prevents a full holiday, why not opt for a short break?

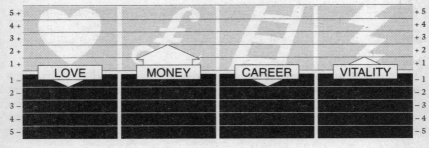

18 MONDAY   *Moon Age Day 12   Moon Sign Sagittarius*

am . . . .

pm . . . .
You can take advantage of a strong competitive edge as the new working
week gets started, though this might not be enough on its own to ensure
outright success. What you also need is the support of people who think
you are equal to the task. Getting them round to your way of thinking
really should not be too difficult.

19 TUESDAY   *Moon Age Day 13   Moon Sign Sagittarius*

am . . . .

pm . . . .
You need to do things to please yourself today, even if that means
upsetting someone else. It is a certainty that you won't get very far by
projecting all your concern towards others. Unless you are also contented
with your lot, it is impossible for you to give your best. For this reason
alone some selfishness is advisable now.

20 WEDNESDAY   *Moon Age Day 14   Moon Sign Capricorn*

am . . . .

pm . . . .
There are signs that challenges and even confrontations at work are what
you relish the most. Some of these could leave colleagues quaking in their
shoes, but not you. Born under the most dominant of the zodiac signs,
you are equal to just about any task and needn't take no for an answer if
you think someone is wrong.

21 THURSDAY   *Moon Age Day 15   Moon Sign Capricorn*

am . . . .

pm . . . .
The present position of Venus in your solar chart could prove to be a
positive boost in terms of friendships. Now your pals are worth a great
deal to you and there is strong evidence that you would go a long way to
support them. Loyalty is one of your key attributes – as long as it suits
your purposes too.

22 FRIDAY
Moon Age Day 16   Moon Sign Aquarius

am . . . .

pm . . . .
Trends suggest that your professional life may now drop back to the slow lane. There isn't much you can do about this situation until the far side of the weekend, which is why the weekend probably starts here for you. It would be more profitable to concentrate on having a good time, rather than flogging a dead horse at work.

23 SATURDAY ☿
Moon Age Day 17   Moon Sign Aquarius

am . . . .

pm . . . .
Today can be very rewarding, though you do need to be careful about what areas of life you choose to highlight. Social trends are especially positive, and you ought to enjoy spending time in the company of good friends. Anything sporting is ideal, as would be a total change of scene and a journey of some sort.

24 SUNDAY ☿
Moon Age Day 18   Moon Sign Pisces

am . . . .

pm . . . .
Venus has now entered your solar sixth house. Together with other planetary trends this inclines you to advance thinking and bestows upon you the ability to make gains as a result of your very good relationships with others. You can seem particularly convincing at present and there is no doubt that you are knowledgeable.

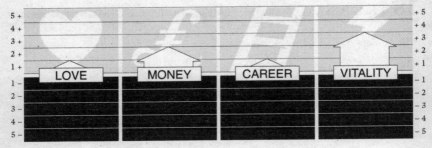

25 MONDAY ☿ *Moon Age Day 19   Moon Sign Pisces*

am . . . .

pm . . . .
Since you are inclined to take yourself and your attributes very much for granted today, it probably isn't too surprising that you find other people doing the same thing. At least your creative potential is good and that allows you to get something looking just right at home or in the environment where you work.

26 TUESDAY ☿ *Moon Age Day 20   Moon Sign Aries*

am . . . .

pm . . . .
The lunar high offers a way out of certain traps you seem to have been setting yourself recently. Confidence is especially high and you have everything it takes to get ahead on several different fronts at the same time. By all means make yourself the centre of attention, but don't do anything to inspire jealousy in others.

27 WEDNESDAY ☿ *Moon Age Day 21   Moon Sign Aries*

am . . . .

pm . . . .
There is an instinctive sense that you are making the right decisions today, which means getting things right first time and avoiding complications later. Your intellect is crystal clear and it would take someone pretty special to fool you at the moment. In almost any situation, you can afford to strike whilst the iron is hot.

28 THURSDAY ☿ *Moon Age Day 22   Moon Sign Taurus*

am . . . .

pm . . . .
There is a powerful impulse to do things right, and since your social conscience is potentially aroused at this time, much of what you get through is on behalf of others. Energy is around in abundance and the progressive nature of the lunar high is still in your mind and showing in your actions.

29 FRIDAY ☿ *Moon Age Day 23   Moon Sign Taurus*

am . . . .

pm . . . .
Patience is the watchword in money matters and this means you would be wise to keep your purse or pocket tightly closed for now. There are better opportunities coming along later and in any case you don't need money in order to have a good time at the moment. Plan now for a weekend that can be both stimulating and very different.

30 SATURDAY ☿ *Moon Age Day 24   Moon Sign Gemini*

am . . . .

pm . . . .
A new interest could turn out to be particularly inspiring, even if it is one that probably has no direct practical relevance to your everyday life. Everyone needs a hobby, though in your case these tend to be related to your success. A complete change of scene is sometimes good for you.

31 SUNDAY ☿ *Moon Age Day 25   Moon Sign Gemini*

am . . . .

pm . . . .
This is an excellent time to let the world know what a big personality you have. Stay away from those who seem to have it in their minds to throw a spanner in the works for you, or at the very least refuse to rise to their bait. Instead, why not concentrate on enjoying yourself and find ways to cheer up those who are less happy at present?

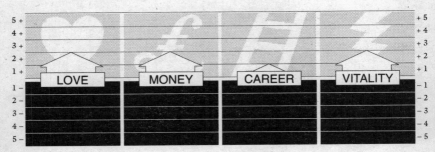

August 2005

YOUR MONTH AT A GLANCE

⊕ = Opportunities are around ⊖ = Be on the defensive ◯ = Life is pretty ordinary

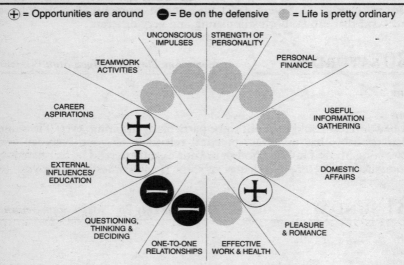

- UNCONSCIOUS IMPULSES
- STRENGTH OF PERSONALITY
- TEAMWORK ACTIVITIES
- PERSONAL FINANCE
- CAREER ASPIRATIONS
- USEFUL INFORMATION GATHERING
- EXTERNAL INFLUENCES/ EDUCATION
- DOMESTIC AFFAIRS
- QUESTIONING, THINKING & DECIDING
- PLEASURE & ROMANCE
- ONE-TO-ONE RELATIONSHIPS
- EFFECTIVE WORK & HEALTH

AUGUST HIGHS AND LOWS

Here I show you how the rhythms of the Moon will affect you this month. Like the tide, your energies and abilities will rise and fall with its pattern. When it is above the centre line, go for it, when it is below, you should be resting.

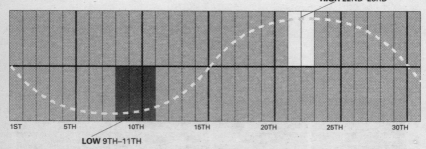

HIGH 22ND–23RD

1ST   5TH   10TH   15TH   20TH   25TH   30TH

LOW 9TH–11TH

1 MONDAY   ☿   *Moon Age Day 26   Moon Sign Gemini*

am . . . .

pm . . . .

On the ideas level you should benefit from new input as the day advances. There is plenty to occupy your mind, in fact too much at times. You would definitely gain if you are willing to listen to the help and advice that comes from people who are in the know. Conforming to expectations can be difficult.

2 TUESDAY   ☿   *Moon Age Day 27   Moon Sign Cancer*

am . . . .

pm . . . .

This may be a good time for winding down certain interests and for replacing them with others. Even if you are getting on well with virtually everyone, there are likely to be one or two people around who present you with specific difficulties. You may need to formulate a special strategy in their case.

3 WEDNESDAY   ☿   *Moon Age Day 28   Moon Sign Cancer*

am . . . .

pm . . . .

A new boost to your love life comes along now that Mercury is in your solar fifth house. Actually speaking words of love becomes easier and you should leave the object of your affections in little doubt about the way you feel. Practical matters may be a little more difficult to address, especially early in the day.

4 THURSDAY   ☿   *Moon Age Day 0   Moon Sign Leo*

am . . . .

pm . . . .

Your quick thinking could prove to be invaluable in matters associated with work. Others quite naturally turn to you for help or advice at present and you should have little difficulty controlling a number of events at the same time. You can allow your confidence to grow as you discover just how many capabilities you possess.

109

5 FRIDAY ☿ *Moon Age Day 1 Moon Sign Leo*

am . . . .

pm . . . .
You could easily benefit from being in the spotlight right now, a position that seems very comfortable to you. Some jobs have to be done in bits but you are able to keep track of a number of tasks and can show just how capable you are. This is the practical, workhorse part of the month and you have what it takes to excel.

6 SATURDAY ☿ *Moon Age Day 2 Moon Sign Leo*

am . . . .

pm . . . .
Your efficiency is still well marked and because it is so obvious, this is how you can impress others. Although you might not advance in any tangible way right now, it is possible that you are being watched by someone. This is as relevant during your social time as it may be whilst you are engaged in your professional activities.

7 SUNDAY ☿ *Moon Age Day 3 Moon Sign Virgo*

am . . . .

pm . . . .
Socially speaking, the pace of your present life shows no tendency to slow down or to become less interesting. What might get on your nerves a little today is other people trying to lord it over you, particularly if the individuals in question have no more idea than you have how to proceed in a specific situation.

8 MONDAY ☿ *Moon Age Day 4   Moon Sign Virgo*

am . . . .

pm . . . .
A certain issue could be causing some confusion to you right now and it might be sensible to seek the advice of someone who has more experience than you do. This is not an admission of guilt on your part and is merely a sensible precaution. Matters of love could continue to occupy your mind for at least part of the day.

9 TUESDAY ☿ *Moon Age Day 5   Moon Sign Libra*

am . . . .

pm . . . .
If you are not careful today you run the risk of scattering your energies too much. You may well decide to settle for second best in a family sense, if only for the sake of peace and quiet. But you need to consider whether this is the right course of action to take, since you are storing up further problems for yourself at a later time.

10 WEDNESDAY ☿ *Moon Age Day 6   Moon Sign Libra*

am . . . .

pm . . . .
The planetary lull patch, caused by the continuing lunar low, comes at a time you could quite well have done without it. As a result you show a tendency to push forward against insurmountable odds. It would be far better to relax for a couple of days and to see what happens later. Patience really is a virtue today.

11 THURSDAY ☿ *Moon Age Day 7   Moon Sign Libra*

am . . . .

pm . . . .
A little self-indulgence seems in order at the moment. There may be little you can do to push forward your own interests and you might only become frustrated if you try too hard. A day to keep an open mind about family issues and to trust younger people to find their own way through a slightly sticky situation.

12 FRIDAY ☿ *Moon Age Day 8 Moon Sign Scorpio*

am . . . .

pm . . . .
There may be significant demands on your time, some of which could have come about as a result of an enforced three-day easing of the pressure. There is a possibility that you are pushing yourself hard and may not get the relaxation that is still vital to you. Look for help and support in some areas of life because it is present.

13 SATURDAY ☿ *Moon Age Day 9 Moon Sign Scorpio*

am . . . .

pm . . . .
If recent delays are still having a knock-on effect, this means having to pace yourself at the start of the weekend. Maybe when you have the time to think about things fully you will realise that much of what you are trying to do is duplication of effort. By the evening you might have convinced yourself to relax.

14 SUNDAY ☿ *Moon Age Day 10 Moon Sign Sagittarius*

am . . . .

pm . . . .
With your ego energy now potentially much stronger, and since the dynamic qualities of Aries are beginning to show themselves more fully, this Sunday might be anything but relaxing. You can afford to enjoy the cut and thrust of life and should be charging forward towards some important destinations.

	LOVE	MONEY	CAREER	VITALITY
5 +				+5
4 +				+4
3 +				+3
2 +				+2
1 +				+1
1 -				-1
2 -				-2
3 -				-3
4 -				-4
5 -				-5

15 MONDAY   ☿ *Moon Age Day 11*   *Moon Sign Sagittarius*

am . . . .

pm . . . .
This would be an excellent time for travel. Those Aries people who have chosen to take a holiday right now have probably made the right decision. You relish fresh places and new faces, so much so that there is a strong chance of making important new friends around now. Confidence has rarely been higher.

16 TUESDAY   *Moon Age Day 12*   *Moon Sign Capricorn*

am . . . .

pm . . . .
If possible, your life could well get even busier from a social point of view. It is worth taking a few moments out of your day from time to time in order to ensure that your partner is not feeling left out of situations. Aries can become very single-minded, occasionally to the detriment of those who are truly important.

17 WEDNESDAY   *Moon Age Day 13*   *Moon Sign Capricorn*

am . . . .

pm . . . .
In professional matters you have what it takes to move ahead at a pace, leaving yourself with the feeling that progress is inevitable at this time. The more confidence you have, the greater is your potential for ultimate success. This may be the most progressive phase you have encountered at any time during this year so far.

18 THURSDAY   *Moon Age Day 14*   *Moon Sign Aquarius*

am . . . .

pm . . . .
Venus now enters your solar seventh house, which is clearly a tonic for any aspect of relationships. Even if you decide to put on a show for the sake of important people who are entering your life at this time, in reality what people are looking for is the real and unvarnished you.

19 FRIDAY

Moon Age Day 15   Moon Sign Aquarius

·am . . . .

pm . . . .
Be careful that no impatient actions on your part upset the natural
equilibrium of the day. There are some matters that are best left the way
they are, whilst interference will only cause difficulties. Half the time now
your best approach is simply to sit back and watch situations unfold.

20 SATURDAY

Moon Age Day 16   Moon Sign Pisces

am . . . .

pm . . . .
Personal considerations inevitably have a bearing on your thinking and
actions this weekend. Things generally could slow a little because the
Moon is in your solar twelfth house. This allows time for relaxation and
for spending precious moments with those who have the most important
part to play in your life.

21 SUNDAY

Moon Age Day 17   Moon Sign Pisces

am . . . .

pm . . . .
Another generally steady sort of day and one during which the potential
for excitement is at a minimum. Without realising why, you would rather
spend time walking on a deserted beach than riding the roller coaster.
Although this is only an interlude, the pause for reflection is almost
certainly going to do you good.

22 MONDAY

Moon Age Day 18   Moon Sign Aries

am . . . .

pm . . . .

You certainly needn't be reluctant to take any sort of gamble as the Moon arrives in your sign. This is the time of the month during which you can afford to take responsibility for your own actions and a period for being very decisive. There will be opponents about, but you can take these in your stride and actually relish the challenge.

23 TUESDAY

Moon Age Day 19   Moon Sign Aries

am . . . .

pm . . . .

Another very responsive day and one on which you may be called upon to do something that has not been in your experience before. This should present little or no problem and you are able to show the world what you are capable of. Relationships should work especially well in the light of your present attitude.

24 WEDNESDAY

Moon Age Day 20   Moon Sign Taurus

am . . . .

pm . . . .

Things tend to turn out well on a material level, even if you don't have quite the same strength of personality that was the case yesterday. Don't argue for your limitations or you are sure to find them. Going for gold in sporting endeavours could boost your ego, though you may have to settle for silver.

25 THURSDAY

Moon Age Day 21   Moon Sign Taurus

am . . . .

pm . . . .

The best thing you can do today is to keep busy. With few restrictions, the degree of headway you can make is well marked, whilst you could discover a few allies you didn't know you had. Your social conscience is high and you might utilise this to confront issues that have to do with your community in some way.

26 FRIDAY
Moon Age Day 22   Moon Sign Gemini

am . . . .

pm . . . .
Trends suggest that your mental processes are swift and you don't show any tendency to slow down. This might be something of a mistake, because a few minutes today contemplating the results of your actions would be more than worthwhile. Keep an open mind about family issues and don't be too authoritarian with younger people.

27 SATURDAY
Moon Age Day 23   Moon Sign Gemini

am . . . .

pm . . . .
Any cheery mood in Aries at the moment might prove to be distinctly infectious. The lighter and more fun-loving qualities of your nature are very much to the fore and you can become the natural joker in any company you keep. By the end of the day there is a possibility you will be seeing old issues in a new way.

28 SUNDAY
Moon Age Day 24   Moon Sign Gemini

am . . . .

pm . . . .
This is not an ideal day to concentrate on working issues. On the contrary, you have scope to go out and have fun. Finding people to join in should be far from difficult and it is clear that you are well liked and deeply respected. In terms of your own ego these factors should prove to be extremely important.

29 MONDAY   *Moon Age Day 25   Moon Sign Cancer*

am . . . .

pm . . . .
Family and home can offer respite on a day when you may not be quite
as keen to push forward as has recently been the case. Even sticking to
routines has its own merit at the start of this working week. Any major
decisions on the professional front may need to be shelved if you decide
to enjoy domestic issues more.

30 TUESDAY   *Moon Age Day 26   Moon Sign Cancer*

am . . . .

pm . . . .
The current period is useful in terms of firming up securities and deciding
what course of action would be best for the future. In many respects you
are rather mellow at this time and more than anxious to show what you
are capable off in terms of long-term forward planning. Why not seek the
encouragement of your partner?

31 WEDNESDAY   *Moon Age Day 27   Moon Sign Leo*

am . . . .

pm . . . .
You are in a position to fulfil your desire for enjoyment and in particular
for romance today. The Moon is in your solar fifth house, assisting you
to find the right words to make others feel at ease and to offer them
greater confidence in themselves. Creative potential is good so house
renovations may be on the cards.

1 THURSDAY   *Moon Age Day 28   Moon Sign Leo*

am . . . .

pm . . . .
You can get much of your own way with others today, whilst at the same
time convincing them that they are at the helm. Don't be too quick to
jump to conclusions and be aware that not everything is quite what it
might seem to be. Arguments in your vicinity are unlikely to be your
concern, so you would be wise to stay out of them.

2 FRIDAY

Moon Age Day 29   Moon Sign Leo

am ....

pm ....
A wonderful time for social harmony and for showing the softer side of
your nature. This caring Aries isn't always on display but it's something
that others love to see. Rules and regulations seem easier to follow at this
time and you can ensure that most people find you approachable,
considerate and fair.

3 SATURDAY

Moon Age Day 0   Moon Sign Virgo

am ....

pm ....
You can certainly make great strides at work, allowing you to prove
yourself in areas that were not your forte before. It is quite possible that
you will be strengthening your position at work and maybe looking at
advancement. Even a total change of professional scene isn't entirely out
of the question.

4 SUNDAY

Moon Age Day 1   Moon Sign Virgo

am ....

pm ....
A favourable period for joint affairs now begins. Venus in your solar
seventh house makes it possible for you to join forces with like-minded
individuals and to approach issues that would have been difficult to
address on your own. There may be disputes around you, but once again
you should avoid joining in with them.

September 2005

YOUR MONTH AT A GLANCE

⊕ = Opportunities are around   ⊖ = Be on the defensive   ● = Life is pretty ordinary

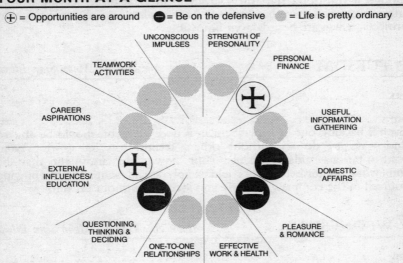

UNCONSCIOUS IMPULSES

STRENGTH OF PERSONALITY

TEAMWORK ACTIVITIES

PERSONAL FINANCE

CAREER ASPIRATIONS

USEFUL INFORMATION GATHERING

EXTERNAL INFLUENCES/ EDUCATION

DOMESTIC AFFAIRS

QUESTIONING, THINKING & DECIDING

PLEASURE & ROMANCE

ONE-TO-ONE RELATIONSHIPS

EFFECTIVE WORK & HEALTH

SEPTEMBER HIGHS AND LOWS

Here I show you how the rhythms of the Moon will affect you this month. Like the tide, your energies and abilities will rise and fall with its pattern. When it is above the centre line, go for it, when it is below, you should be resting.

HIGH 18TH–19TH

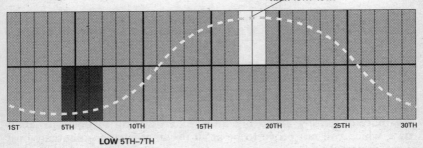

1ST   5TH   10TH   15TH   20TH   25TH   30TH

LOW 5TH–7TH

119

5 MONDAY
Moon Age Day 2   Moon Sign Libra

am . . . .

pm . . . .
You would be wise to slow down the current pace of events whilst the
lunar low is around. Getting to where you want to be can be difficult,
though if you don't start the journey in the first place, leaving it until
later, frustration may be avoided. This applies just as much to new
projects, which are best delayed if possible.

6 TUESDAY
Moon Age Day 3   Moon Sign Libra

am . . . .

pm . . . .
Even if backing out of a specific plan is necessary, you should be able to
find ways to do so without others feeling too let down. Avoid
confrontations today, because your powers of argument may be
somewhat diminished. You could simply spend some hours enjoying
yourself in the company of those you love and without pressure.

7 WEDNESDAY
Moon Age Day 4   Moon Sign Libra

am . . . .

pm . . . .
Although it would be advisable to be circumspect early in the day, later
on your accustomed vigour could well begin to return. Beware of taking
too many chances at work, though by the time the evening comes along
you may once again be the life and soul of just about any party. Plan now
for a trip late in September.

8 THURSDAY
Moon Age Day 5   Moon Sign Scorpio

am . . . .

pm . . . .
A phase of high energies and significant output is now upon you. The
Sun is in your solar sixth house, offering new opportunities and the
possibility of getting ahead big time. Avoid getting involved in family
rows, which will not prove to be at all useful at such a potentially busy
and committed time.

120

9 FRIDAY

Moon Age Day 6   Moon Sign Scorpio

am ....

pm ....
Making progress today may be as dependent on others as on your own nature. If colleagues or friends are not coming good with their promises, your best response is to turn your attention in a different direction and be willing to modify your plans. A day to stay right away from boring routines in which you achieve next to nothing.

10 SATURDAY

Moon Age Day 7   Moon Sign Sagittarius

am ....

pm ....
There are signs that changes to the smooth running of your life now seem necessary and you need to show just how adaptable you are capable of being. Standing up for yourself in situations of conflict certainly isn't difficult, though whether it proves to be absolutely necessary does remain to be seen. Stay circumspect.

11 SUNDAY

Moon Age Day 8   Moon Sign Sagittarius

am ....

pm ....
Normal service is resumed, after a day or two during which it is possible that the problems of others have fallen into your lap. This can be a busy and active Sunday and a time during which you could be wearing a number of different hats. Aries people who work at the weekend can get on especially well now.

12 MONDAY
Moon Age Day 9   Moon Sign Capricorn

am ....

pm ....
Emotional relationships tend to thrive on intimacy at this stage. As a result, you may choose to be close to that very special person. Conforming to expectations in a practical sense could well be a problem. However, people should accept your peculiarities if you see them yourself and remain humorous about them.

13 TUESDAY
Moon Age Day 10   Moon Sign Capricorn

am ....

pm ....
Professionally speaking, you have what it takes to be ready for just about any challenge that now comes your way. What might be less satisfying is dealing with the general dross. Where possible, seek the help of someone who is better with routine work than you are. Aries wants to be in the driving seat big time at present.

14 WEDNESDAY
Moon Age Day 11   Moon Sign Aquarius

am ....

pm ....
Even if you are feeling quite generous today, it is important not to give away too much. In particular, you would be wise to keep your innovative ideas to yourself because there is some practical mileage in them in the fullness of time. Once again you may well run up against rules and regulations you see as being pointless.

15 THURSDAY
Moon Age Day 12   Moon Sign Aquarius

am ....

pm ....
Social groups and co-operative ventures have a great deal to offer you today, so much so that more practical considerations are likely to be taking a back seat. Creative potential is also good, and together with those around you, there is a strong possibility that you want to make significant changes on the home front.

16 FRIDAY
Moon Age Day 13   Moon Sign Pisces

am . . . .

pm . . . .
Intimate relationships are what now make life really worth living, even if something else has to take second place in order to make way for them. Pleasing your loved ones makes you happy too and you tend to go through life with a definite smile on your face at this time. Confidence remains essentially high.

17 SATURDAY
Moon Age Day 14   Moon Sign Pisces

am . . . .

pm . . . .
You could well afford to be a little more ambitious right now, particularly if your love affair with the more personal aspects of life is temporarily over. These switches in emphasis are not at all unusual for Aries and you have the ability to respond to them in a very philosophical manner, as fortunately does everyone else.

18 SUNDAY
Moon Age Day 15   Moon Sign Aries

am . . . .

pm . . . .
This should be one of the best days of the month in a holistic sense, though the fact that that lunar high comes along at the weekend won't be an advantage to all Aries subjects. You may not be able to get the things done you would wish and are likely to meet just a few minor frustrations if you try in any case.

19 MONDAY

Moon Age Day 16   Moon Sign Aries

am . . . .

pm . . . .
This is the best time for making new starts and for taking advantage of situations you see as being in your best interests. Don't take no for an answer, especially in a professional sense. September is, in any case, just about the best month of the year for getting what you want in a practical and financial way.

20 TUESDAY

Moon Age Day 17   Moon Sign Taurus

am . . . .

pm . . . .
Some great discussions are possible at present, and you seem to be the person who is inspiring the majority of them. You could find yourself up against it when it comes to the requirements of life. This being the case, you might once again decide to call upon the help and support of others.

21 WEDNESDAY

Moon Age Day 18   Moon Sign Taurus

am . . . .

pm . . . .
Fortune favours the brave, which of course includes all Aries subjects. Don't wait around to be invited to do anything today. You have what it takes to decide what you want from life and go out to get it. Confidences have to be kept, especially when they involve friends who have been a part of your life for years.

22 THURSDAY

Moon Age Day 19   Moon Sign Taurus

am . . . .

pm . . . .
On the whole this has potential to be a busy period on the financial front and it may not offer you quite the time you would wish for the niceties of life. If you explain to those you care for why you are so busy, they should understand. To show this consideration would not take very much at all out of your day.

23 FRIDAY — *Moon Age Day 20   Moon Sign Gemini*

am . . . .

pm . . . .
Personal relationships continue to be highlighted, and to offer a sense of
'rightness' that may not come from other spheres of your life. Sporting
Aries subjects ought to be right in their element today and can find ways
to mix their physical exercise with professional demands. Beware of being
too quick to jump to any conclusion.

24 SATURDAY — *Moon Age Day 21   Moon Sign Gemini*

am . . . .

pm . . . .
You should benefit from continued freedom of movement and probably
won't be too keen to be tied to a routine you find in any way restricting.
Confidence is high but can be somewhat dented if you are told outright
that something you believe is downright wrong. These are situations you
simply have to take on the chin.

25 SUNDAY — *Moon Age Day 22   Moon Sign Cancer*

am . . . .

pm . . . .
Trends indicate that new information is coming in all the time this
weekend, though some of it won't be put to good use until later in the
week. All the same, it's worth keeping your ears and eyes open, because
even apparent coincidences can turn out to be much more in the fullness
of time. The attitude of a friend could be puzzling.

26 MONDAY
Moon Age Day 23   Moon Sign Cancer

am . . . .

pm . . . .
A powerful focus on family life now comes from the position of the
Moon in your solar fourth house. This lunar position stays solid for a
couple of days, making this the best time to talk to relatives about almost
anything. A sentimental streak is evident, something that Aries is not
exactly famous for.

27 TUESDAY
Moon Age Day 24   Moon Sign Cancer

am . . . .

pm . . . .
Be careful when it comes to making financial decisions because it appears
that your mind is not working quite as clearly today as has been the case
earlier in the month. It might be best to leave any large amounts of
spending until a later date. For now, simply sitting back and enjoying
some of the good things of life would be no bad thing.

28 WEDNESDAY
Moon Age Day 25   Moon Sign Leo

am . . . .

pm . . . .
You now have scope to ensure that material concerns go your way again,
though these don't seem half as important in the full light of a romantic
glow that surrounds you at present. Leave a few tasks until later and
spend time in the arms of someone very special. Even a lacklustre
attachment can be burnished to perfection at this time.

29 THURSDAY
Moon Age Day 26   Moon Sign Leo

am . . . .

pm . . . .
Your personal charm is in evidence and the world isn't tardy when it
comes to recognising the fact. Creating the right impression should not
be at all difficult and it becomes obvious that you are firing on all
cylinders in the popularity stakes. Attitude is all-important, as you should
realise today.

30 FRIDAY   *Moon Age Day 27   Moon Sign Virgo*

am . . . .

pm . . . .
The present position of Mercury is excellent for communications of almost any sort. Although you could find that specific people are awkward to deal with, in a general sense you shouldn't have any difficulty adapting your nature to suit the person and the moment. Everything seems fresh and clean under current trends.

1 SATURDAY   *Moon Age Day 28   Moon Sign Virgo*

am . . . .

pm . . . .
You may find you are on the go from morning until night, which isn't exactly appealing at the weekend. This probably isn't the case with you at the moment because you are achieving so much and will be happy to stay out there in the mainstream. Helping others comes more or less naturally today.

2 SUNDAY   *Moon Age Day 0   Moon Sign Virgo*

am . . . .

pm . . . .
Well-meaning emotional support from others shouldn't be at all difficult to find, though whether or not you really want it is open to doubt. Try to stay cool about the situation and listen to what they have to say. After all, you don't have to take their advice and will most probably do what suits you best in any case.

October 2005

YOUR MONTH AT A GLANCE

⊕ = Opportunities are around   ⊖ = Be on the defensive   ⬤ = Life is pretty ordinary

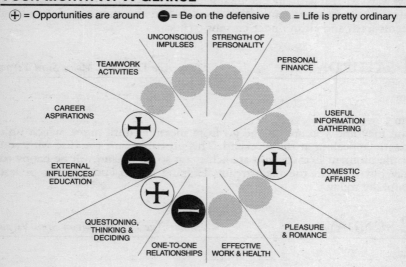

OCTOBER HIGHS AND LOWS

Here I show you how the rhythms of the Moon will affect you this month. Like the tide, your energies and abilities will rise and fall with its pattern. When it is above the centre line, go for it, when it is below, you should be resting.

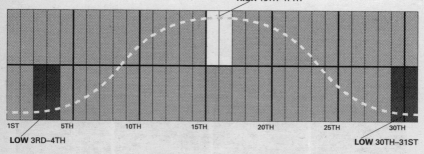

HIGH 16TH–17TH

1ST   5TH   10TH   15TH   20TH   25TH   30TH

LOW 3RD–4TH

LOW 30TH–31ST

3 MONDAY   *Moon Age Day 1   Moon Sign Libra*

am . . . .

pm . . . .
General energies are likely to be flagging at this time, thanks to the lunar
low, which is why you might deliberately choose to take a rest.
Conforming to the expectations of others is hardest of all, but you will
probably be retreating into your shell somewhat in any case. Mechanical
things could seem to be working against you at present.

4 TUESDAY   *Moon Age Day 2   Moon Sign Libra*

am . . . .

pm . . . .
Your best approach today is to keep demands to a minimum and
concentrate on doing what you really want. You can't expect to get ahead
for now, and so would do better looking at past efforts and planning new
ones. Call upon others for support in matters you aren't sure about, and
in particular rely on family members.

5 WEDNESDAY   *Moon Age Day 3   Moon Sign Scorpio*

am . . . .

pm . . . .
As the autumn winds begin to blow you might decide on one last trip
before the end of the year. There are great opportunities about and it
seems important at present to please yourself, though you might have to
take the needs and wants of family members on board too.

6 THURSDAY   *Moon Age Day 4   Moon Sign Scorpio*

am . . . .

pm . . . .
Where practical matters are concerned it is evident right now that you
want to do things in more or less your own way. You are creative and
keen to get ahead, even if not all trends seem to be going your way. What
you possess at the moment is the ability to push over obstacles wherever
they appear.

7 FRIDAY
Moon Age Day 5   Moon Sign Sagittarius

am . . . .

pm . . . .
An entire change of scene would probably do you good, and there are few issues that need resolving so badly that you can't take a break. You would come back refreshed and better able to see the wood for the trees. Take special note of any romantic proposals that come your way at or around this time.

8 SATURDAY
Moon Age Day 6   Moon Sign Sagittarius

am . . . .

pm . . . .
Venus is still in your solar eighth house and this powerful influence is likely to have a great bearing on relationships of a personal nature, as well as important friendships. It is possible you are thinking about things differently now, and will want to air your views to the people concerned, that is if they will stay around to listen.

9 SUNDAY
Moon Age Day 7   Moon Sign Sagittarius

am . . . .

pm . . . .
Trends now benefit partnerships, whether they are of a practical, professional or personal nature. Seeing the other person's point of view isn't always your strong point, but seems to be much more so at present. Routines are for the birds this Sunday and you can afford to insist on doing whatever comes into your mind.

10 MONDAY
Moon Age Day 8   Moon Sign Capricorn

am . . . .

pm . . . .
There might now be greater opportunity for self-determined success. Although you are subject to certain rules and regulations, you don't seem to be in the sort of frame of mind that takes these facts on board. Access to people who are in the know is open to you for the next few days, and there are gains to be made if you use it.

11 TUESDAY
Moon Age Day 9   Moon Sign Capricorn

am . . . .

pm . . . .
You are able to keep the wheels of progress turning nicely, and show a willingness to change with the wind. This isn't always the case with Aries, which can be the most stubborn of all the zodiac signs with the possible exception of Taurus. The signs are that all manner of people fascinate you today, and for a host of different reasons.

12 WEDNESDAY
Moon Age Day 10   Moon Sign Aquarius

am . . . .

pm . . . .
Social affairs allow you to feel more carefree and to come to terms with your general popularity at the moment. Your attitude is good and the sense of humour you are able to display at present is especially strong. There could be one or two things you don't want to do today, and the simple advice is get stuck in and sort them out quickly.

13 THURSDAY
Moon Age Day 11   Moon Sign Aquarius

am . . . .

pm . . . .
The more you are in the company of interesting people today, the greater can be your sense of joy and happiness. Don't confine your interests in any way, but spread yourself across a range of different subjects. Romance is once again showing itself, spurred on by your present light-hearted attitude.

14 FRIDAY
Moon Age Day 12   Moon Sign Pisces

am . . . .

pm . . . .
Time spent alone at the moment would be preferable to finding yourself
at odds with others. Concern for the underdog is strong, but the
necessary energy to do what it takes to sort matters out probably isn't
present. A watershed is at hand when it comes to the way you are
thinking about career prospects in particular.

15 SATURDAY
Moon Age Day 13   Moon Sign Pisces

am . . . .

pm . . . .
There may be some financial complexities to be sorted out today, even if
this doesn't look to be the case during the first part of Saturday. A
shopping spree might suit your present frame of mind and would offer
you the chance to be on the receiving end of a number of potential
bargains well ahead of Christmas.

16 SUNDAY
Moon Age Day 14   Moon Sign Aries

am . . . .

pm . . . .
The Moon returns to your zodiac sign, reinforcing your will and making
it possible to move some sizeable mountains. Whether your personal
circumstances favour this interlude on a Sunday remains to be seen, but
you certainly should not doubt either your own tenacity or your practical
abilities today.

17 MONDAY
Moon Age Day 15   Moon Sign Aries

am . . . .

pm . . . .
This is another excellent time for making fresh starts of almost any sort.
Although you are inspirational in your thinking, you have what it takes
to use your good ideas in a very practical sense. Lady Luck is likely to be
on your side, so some modest speculations might be something you
would consider.

18 TUESDAY
Moon Age Day 16   Moon Sign Taurus

am . . . .

pm . . . .
This is an excellent time to look out anything unusual or even downright
peculiar. Don't doubt your intuition at this stage because it is potentially
strong and unlikely to lead you in the wrong direction. Counting on the
support of a friend might be a mistake, particularly if they are busy and
possibly quite worried at present.

19 WEDNESDAY
Moon Age Day 17   Moon Sign Taurus

am . . . .

pm . . . .
You certainly have your work cut out today if you want to get through
everything that seems to be important. The attitude of friends is still
likely to be rather peculiar, leaving you wondering what you might have
done. By all means give them time, because in the end you should see
that you have no part to play in their present frame of mind.

20 THURSDAY
Moon Age Day 18   Moon Sign Gemini

am . . . .

pm . . . .
You needn't let good ideas languish today simply because you don't seem
to have what it takes to make them work. Instead of taking no for an
answer, why not push your weight around a little? This is not something
that comes hard to Aries and it could ensure you have a positive listening
ear from someone important.

21 FRIDAY
Moon Age Day 19   Moon Sign Gemini

am . . . .

pm . . . .
Trends suggest that close and even intimate involvements have a big part
to play in your thinking today. You may be taking something of a holiday
from routine and will want to turn in the direction of the people you care
about the most. You are in a position to be of direct practical assistance
in more than one case.

22 SATURDAY
Moon Age Day 20   Moon Sign Cancer

am . . . .

pm . . . .
The pace of events seems to slow a little, allowing you the time to pause
and take breath. Because of the present astrological trends you are
unlikely to think in terms of a hellfire sort of weekend. On the contrary,
the lure of a comfortable armchair might seem just too irresistible to
be ignored.

23 SUNDAY
Moon Age Day 21   Moon Sign Cancer

am . . . .

pm . . . .
Despite a slightly quieter frame of mind, social impulses are strong and
the opportunities to mix are there for the taking from a wealth of
different directions. By all means stand up for your rights if you think
they are being ignored, but don't push issues too strongly. You are
capable of being wrong, even if you hate to admit the fact.

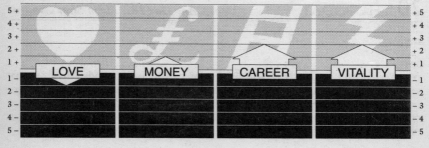

24 MONDAY
Moon Age Day 22   Moon Sign Cancer

am . . . .

pm . . . .
You need to keep a variety of interests on the go now if at all possible. Don't be too quick to make dramatic changes, especially to your professional life. Today needs a gentle touch on the tiller and the certain knowledge that every action you take might have a slightly adverse bearing on others.

25 TUESDAY
Moon Age Day 23   Moon Sign Cancer

am . . . .

pm . . . .
Romance and personal relationships generally should seem quite harmonious today, at a time when you have more time to look at them. By tomorrow, it could well be action all the way again, so you should enjoy the less stressful moments that surround you now. Looking up someone you haven't seen for a while would be no bad thing.

26 WEDNESDAY
Moon Age Day 24   Moon Sign Leo

am . . . .

pm . . . .
Even if you don't want to believe everything you hear today, be cautious, because at least some of it could be true. Confidence is growing all the time in a professional sense, but you can be too clever for your own good. It is important to check and recheck all facts and figures before proceeding with any specific deal.

27 THURSDAY
Moon Age Day 25   Moon Sign Leo

am . . . .

pm . . . .
The further you can reach, the better you should feel today. That doesn't mean you should knock yourself out, which isn't exactly the right recipe for success in the longer term. You need pace and a good deal of common sense if you want to make the most of every opportunity, of which there are many now.

28 FRIDAY

Moon Age Day 26   Moon Sign Virgo

am . . . .

pm . . . .
You could do worse than to stay close to those around you who have real power, particularly at work. Your own ideas are sound, and worth discussing with anyone who is willing to listen. Once work is out of the way, you show a great capacity for simply having a good time.

29 SATURDAY

Moon Age Day 27   Moon Sign Virgo

am . . . .

pm . . . .
There may be emotional ups and downs to be dealt with today, though if you are busy in a practical sense you may not even notice. This could be disconcerting for your partner if they want to address specific issues. A good old-fashioned heart-to-heart talk is probably required and would yield dividends.

30 SUNDAY

Moon Age Day 28   Moon Sign Libra

am . . . .

pm . . . .
A mixture of some confusion and not a little incompetence could be the order of the day unless you show extra care. The Moon isn't doing you any favours in your opposite sign and you really do need to call on the help and support of others in order to get the very best out of today. All in all, it might be best to stay tucked up in bed!

31 MONDAY   *Moon Age Day 29   Moon Sign Libra*

am . . . .

pm . . . .
The lull continues today, though is somewhat mitigated by the present position of the Sun, which is much more helpful to you in the shorter term. All the same, this might be a better time for planning than for putting your schemes into action. Be wary of bargains that look too good to be true. They probably are.

1 TUESDAY   *Moon Age Day 0   Moon Sign Scorpio*

am . . . .

pm . . . .
It appears you prefer a diversity of interests at the start of November. This would certainly seem to be what the present planetary line-up is indicating. However, there may be specific issues that are presently difficult to avoid. Turning your attention towards them probably won't be too appealing, but it could be necessary.

2 WEDNESDAY   *Moon Age Day 1   Moon Sign Scorpio*

am . . . .

pm . . . .
An over-assertive attitude is possible for you today but it won't help any situation. Try to stay as low key as possible because that is the way you are most likely to influence those around you. In a practical sense, a little of this and a bit of that is the way to approach jobs at present.

3 THURSDAY   *Moon Age Day 2   Moon Sign Scorpio*

am . . . .

pm . . . .
The Moon is now in your solar ninth house, which is good if you have to be on the move. You can gain noticeably from fresh fields and pastures new and shouldn't be at all fazed by meeting a varied selection of individuals. Now is the time to confront any petty fears you may have – that's the Aries way to deal with them.

4 FRIDAY
Moon Age Day 3   Moon Sign Sagittarius

am . . . .

pm . . . .
There are some good ideas on the financial front and you would be wise to implement them just as quickly as you can. This is an ideal time for taking any problem by the scruff of the neck and shaking it into order. Don't take no for an answer from someone else, particularly if you have the power to override their opinion gently.

5 SATURDAY
Moon Age Day 4   Moon Sign Sagittarius

am . . . .

pm . . . .
Venus now in your ninth house encourages you to come out of your shell, that is, if you have been in one of late. Most Aries people have a sixth sense when it comes to analysing others, though they employ it all too rarely. Deep feelings need to be listened to right now, especially ones that have a bearing on personal attachments.

6 SUNDAY
Moon Age Day 5   Moon Sign Capricorn

am . . . .

pm . . . .
The signs are that others are looking upon you very favourably now and are not likely to cause you any undue problems. If they have influence, then so much the better. In a home-related sense, you need to be as sensitive as possible if you are not going to accidentally overrule a relative who is genuinely doing their best.

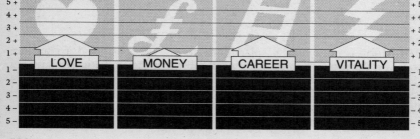

138

November

2005

YOUR MONTH AT A GLANCE

$\oplus$ = Opportunities are around $\ominus$ = Be on the defensive   ● = Life is pretty ordinary

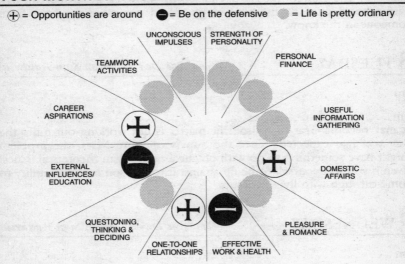

- UNCONSCIOUS IMPULSES
- STRENGTH OF PERSONALITY
- TEAMWORK ACTIVITIES
- PERSONAL FINANCE
- CAREER ASPIRATIONS
- USEFUL INFORMATION GATHERING
- EXTERNAL INFLUENCES/EDUCATION
- DOMESTIC AFFAIRS
- QUESTIONING, THINKING & DECIDING
- PLEASURE & ROMANCE
- ONE-TO-ONE RELATIONSHIPS
- EFFECTIVE WORK & HEALTH

NOVEMBER HIGHS AND LOWS

Here I show you how the rhythms of the Moon will affect you this month. Like the tide, your energies and abilities will rise and fall with its pattern. When it is above the centre line, go for it, when it is below, you should be resting.

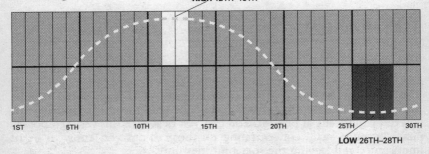

HIGH 12TH–13TH

1ST 5TH 10TH 15TH 20TH 25TH 30TH

LOW 26TH–28TH

7 MONDAY
Moon Age Day 6   Moon Sign Capricorn

am . . . .

pm . . . .
This could prove to be one of the best days of November when it comes to career interests. However, you do need to be careful to diversify when necessary and should not allow yourself to get stuck in any sort of rut. The time is right to listen to some sound professional advice from someone in the know.

8 TUESDAY
Moon Age Day 7   Moon Sign Aquarius

am . . . .

pm . . . .
It may become clear that a specific matter is not working out quite the way you had expected. Since the Sun is opposite Mars, the problem might have something to do with practical rather than theoretical issues. Even if you feel yourself to be up against it today, you have the ability to come through with flying colours.

9 WEDNESDAY
Moon Age Day 8   Moon Sign Aquarius

am . . . .

pm . . . .
A period of transformation is upon you and this is a long-term affair with quite far-reaching implications. It won't be until December that you fully appreciate some of the potentials now developing in your life. A day to avoid arguments at a personal level and simply get on with what is expected of you.

10 THURSDAY
Moon Age Day 9   Moon Sign Pisces

am . . . .

pm . . . .
This may not be the best time for keeping up a high social profile. Although it isn't a common occurrence for you, there is a tendency for you to be quite shy at present. You can best deal with this very temporary phase by once again concentrating on those things you know to be of importance and leaving the social niceties until later.

11 FRIDAY

Moon Age Day 10   Moon Sign Pisces

am . . . .

pm . . . .

Now on a personal voyage of discovery, don't be at all surprised if some facts and figures come in that give you a greater understanding of the way the world works. With a renewed sense of wonder and plenty of opportunity, today could be rather special, if somewhat odd.

12 SATURDAY

Moon Age Day 11   Moon Sign Aries

am . . . .

pm . . . .

The lunar high arrives, and you needn't allow anyone to talk you out of something that seems personally important. Other people have their own agendas, which are not the same as yours. Be willing to compromise over family matters, whilst at the same time keeping to your own agenda in the more practical areas of life.

13 SUNDAY

Moon Age Day 12   Moon Sign Aries

am . . . .

pm . . . .

A day to put your persuasive tongue to good use and concentrate on forging ahead. The lunar high brings energy when you need it the most and increases your powers of communication. Stamina is the greatest gift offered by this period and your staying power should be much increased.

14 MONDAY ☿ *Moon Age Day 13   Moon Sign Taurus*

am . . . .

pm . . . .
There is a great deal of help on offer when it comes to professional
developments. All the same, you may also be quite occupied with home-
based issues and might have to spend a part of the day convincing family
members that your point of view is the most valid. Beware of being too
quick to take offence in simple discussions.

15 TUESDAY ☿ *Moon Age Day 14   Moon Sign Taurus*

am . . . .

pm . . . .
Your desire is strongly emphasised at the moment and the deeply romantic
qualities of Aries begin to show. Don't rush matters that you know to be
important, even if you can hardly avoid being impulsive at present. Slow
and steady wins any race – a fact you should now appreciate.

16 WEDNESDAY ☿ *Moon Age Day 15   Moon Sign Taurus*

am . . . .

pm . . . .
News from far off could prove to be a good stimulus to your personal life.
Maybe someone you haven't heard from for ages is getting in touch
again, offering you a journey or planning one. At work your best
approach is to show a very positive face to new opportunities, even if you
have doubts about them.

17 THURSDAY ☿ *Moon Age Day 16   Moon Sign Gemini*

am . . . .

pm . . . .
This is a day when you really will have to put your versatility to good use.
Almost any sphere of life could grab your attention and you won't really
be much of a specialist at the moment. Comfort and security, though at
the back of your mind, might not come to the forefront at such a
potentially busy time as this.

18 FRIDAY ☿ *Moon Age Day 17 Moon Sign Gemini*

am . . . .

pm . . . .
This is an ideal time to decide whether you should jettison some aspects of life that are now of little or no use to you. Concentrate on the matter at hand, even though this is likely to be quite difficult. When the practicalities are out of the way, you can afford to make the most of very favourable social and romantic trends.

19 SATURDAY ☿ *Moon Age Day 18 Moon Sign Cancer*

am . . . .

pm . . . .
What you hear on the grapevine today could be just as important as what you are being told directly. It is a combination of the two that allows you to make up your own mind for the future. This may be just as well, particularly if there are people around you now who are deliberately dealing in misinformation.

20 SUNDAY ☿ *Moon Age Day 19 Moon Sign Cancer*

am . . . .

pm . . . .
This is a Sunday and so it wouldn't be surprising if you were to find yourself in the bosom of your family. Part of your nature will be pleased about this, though there may still be a burning desire inside you to address issues that are less likely to be resolved at the weekend. Try to be patient and enjoy family times.

21 MONDAY ☿ *Moon Age Day 20   Moon Sign Leo*

am . . . .

pm . . . .
You would be wise to listen out for news regarding personal aspirations
and wishes. With a great deal of potential joy in your life you have what
it takes to push forward towards specific horizons with much energy and
enthusiasm. In terms of personal happiness, this could be one of the best
days of the month.

22 TUESDAY ☿ *Moon Age Day 21   Moon Sign Leo*

am . . . .

pm . . . .
You may be too busy to worry much about money in a day-to-day sense
and yet it is very important to do so. Those Aries subjects who take a
responsible attitude to life will already be planning for Christmas and
today would be fine for shopping or for looking carefully at exactly what
is available to spend.

23 WEDNESDAY ☿ *Moon Age Day 22   Moon Sign Leo*

am . . . .

pm . . . .
The time is right to seize on whatever opportunities are available, and not
to be tardy when it comes to getting what you want from life in a
professional sense. Meanwhile, you should find that domestic matters are
pleasant and satisfying. Rely on the special support that comes from
much-valued friends of long standing.

24 THURSDAY ☿ *Moon Age Day 23   Moon Sign Virgo*

am . . . .

pm . . . .
You can make this another day of satisfactory accomplishments, even if
situations are not as clear-cut as you might wish. Even if getting to the
nitty-gritty of specific matters isn't at all easy, you do have it in your
power to show a determined and positive face to issues that you know are
going to be important later.

25 FRIDAY ☿ *Moon Age Day 24   Moon Sign Virgo*

am . . . .

pm . . . .
The sort of information that you can glean from others today should prove to be both interesting and useful, so it is worthwhile keeping your ear to the ground. This is especially true in any situation regarding work. Conforming to expectations in personal matters could be fraught with difficulty, especially if your freedom is at stake.

26 SATURDAY ☿ *Moon Age Day 25   Moon Sign Libra*

am . . . .

pm . . . .
It looks as though this is a time when you need to slow down the action. The lunar low has potential to sap your strength somewhat and to make it difficult for you to see the road ahead quite as clearly as you might wish. The best thing you can do is to sit back and wait. Present trends don't last long and do allow some time to rest.

27 SUNDAY ☿ *Moon Age Day 26   Moon Sign Libra*

am . . . .

pm . . . .
Even if the pace of life remains sluggish, you can do those sort of things that are expected of you at this time of year. Planning for Christmas could be high on the list and your undivided attention for once would probably please your partner or other family members. Not a particularly sparkling day, but useful all the same.

28 MONDAY ☿ *Moon Age Day 27   Moon Sign Libra*

am . . . .

pm . . . .
This would be another favourable time to broaden your horizons, though you probably won't begin doing so until the middle of the day. Trends suggest that creature comforts have less appeal now and that you are willing to go without almost anything in the search to get what you really want from life.

29 TUESDAY ☿ *Moon Age Day 28   Moon Sign Scorpio*

am . . . .

pm . . . .
A matter between yourself and a loved one today can have a strong bearing on your ability to enjoy yourself. You would be wise to pay close attention to emotional issues because they could turn out to be more significant than you think. Friends can be of great importance in the days ahead and you are addressing their needs and wants.

30 WEDNESDAY ☿ *Moon Age Day 29   Moon Sign Scorpio*

am . . . .

pm . . . .
You can now put yourself at the forefront of the action, a position you enjoy the most. Conforming to expectations might not be easy and in fact for most of the time today you may not even bother to do so. With less emphasis on home and family than has been the case for most of November, you can finish the month with a social flourish.

1 THURSDAY ☿ *Moon Age Day 0   Moon Sign Sagittarius*

am . . . .

pm . . . .
It is time to explore the big, wide world beyond your own front door. Although it is late in the year you might opt for travel or for some other diversion that is a million miles away from the everyday considerations of your life. You could well find it difficult to concentrate on some issues at the moment if you have a roving mind.

2 FRIDAY
☿ *Moon Age Day 1* *Moon Sign Sagittarius*

am . . . .

pm . . . .
The Sun is now in your solar ninth house, another generally uplifting trend and one that is going to be with you until just short of Christmas. Mental pursuits and personal encounters could both figure prominently in your day and you might find that your popularity is a great deal more emphasised than you would have expected.

3 SATURDAY
☿ *Moon Age Day 2* *Moon Sign Capricorn*

am . . . .

pm . . . .
There now seems to be a strong accent on physical pleasures, though you may not need to slacken your efforts with regard to work. Loving relationships are quite obvious as places of resort once the working day is over, but you could find certain family members behaving in a less than typical way.

4 SUNDAY
Moon Age Day 3 *Moon Sign Capricorn*

am . . . .

pm . . . .
What seems to matter more than almost anything today is a strong sense of security. This could take many forms, from adding extra bolts to the door, right through to examining your insurance policies. Much of this seems tedious, but you are in the right frame of mind to address such issues on this December Sunday.

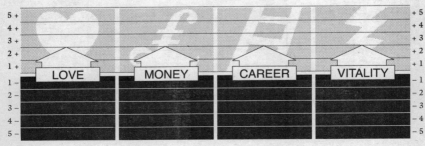

(Aries ♈)

December
2005

YOUR MONTH AT A GLANCE

⊕ = Opportunities are around   ⊖ = Be on the defensive   ⬤ = Life is pretty ordinary

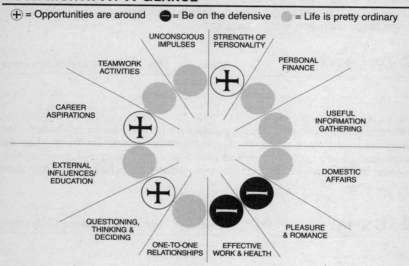

STRENGTH OF PERSONALITY

UNCONSCIOUS IMPULSES

TEAMWORK ACTIVITIES

PERSONAL FINANCE

CAREER ASPIRATIONS

USEFUL INFORMATION GATHERING

EXTERNAL INFLUENCES/ EDUCATION

DOMESTIC AFFAIRS

QUESTIONING, THINKING & DECIDING

ONE-TO-ONE RELATIONSHIPS

EFFECTIVE WORK & HEALTH

PLEASURE & ROMANCE

DECEMBER HIGHS AND LOWS

Here I show you how the rhythms of the Moon will affect you this month. Like the tide, your energies and abilities will rise and fall with its pattern. When it is above the centre line, go for it, when it is below, you should be resting.

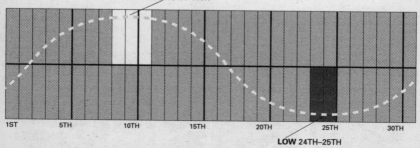

HIGH 9TH–11TH

LOW 24TH–25TH

1ST   5TH   10TH   15TH   20TH   25TH   30TH

148

5 MONDAY *Moon Age Day 4   Moon Sign Aquarius*

am . . . .

pm . . . .
There could be much about today that will enable you to feel generally happy and contented with life. You seem to have temporarily shelved your accustomed need to get ahead at all cost, in favour of sitting back and relaxing, whilst surveying your accomplishments so far this year.

6 TUESDAY *Moon Age Day 5   Moon Sign Aquarius*

am . . . .

pm . . . .
You could well find that your powers of intuition are good and that you can almost instinctively understand the way others are likely to react under any given circumstance. Rules and regulations tend to get on your nerves again, because you always know better than the powers that be!

7 WEDNESDAY *Moon Age Day 6   Moon Sign Pisces*

am . . . .

pm . . . .
Do keep your life as varied as you can and don't be too tied to issues that are of no real importance. It shouldn't be hard for you to cherry-pick at present, opting for those aspects of life that have a fascination for you. Any confusion regarding social or travel details can soon be sorted out.

8 THURSDAY *Moon Age Day 7   Moon Sign Pisces*

am . . . .

pm . . . .
General energies and your need to get ahead are now more to the fore than they were earlier in the week. You have scope to turn your attention to longer-term plans and issues, perhaps alongside like-minded individuals. There are gains to be made at a personal level, though not until the practical requirements of the day are sorted out.

9 FRIDAY
Moon Age Day 8   Moon Sign Aries

am . . . .

pm . . . .
As the Moon enters your sign, influences coming your way in a career
sense are much to the fore. Little things you hear play on your mind and
cause you to look carefully at half-forgotten matters or ones that didn't
look important before. Intuition is strong and ought to tell you when a
potential purchase is really worth the asking price.

10 SATURDAY
Moon Age Day 9   Moon Sign Aries

am . . . .

pm . . . .
This is the most pronounced progressive phase throughout the whole of
December and you won't want to waste it by being in the wrong place.
Now is the time to concentrate on the matter at hand and push all your
energies in a single direction. Despite this need, your mind wanders far
and wide, encompassing many possibilities.

11 SUNDAY
Moon Age Day 10   Moon Sign Aries

am . . . .

pm . . . .
Another good day for putting new projects into action. There could well
be some unusual people about at the moment, some of who have a
specific part to play in your thinking and planning. A change of attitude
becomes possible and this could lead you down paths that were
previously quite unthinkable.

12 MONDAY   *Moon Age Day 11   Moon Sign Taurus*

am . . . .

pm . . . .
Mercury now enters your solar ninth house, bringing a boost to all
mental issues. In terms of communication you can be on top form and
should find it easy to get your message across. Neither are you forgetting
the needs of your personal life. Dishing out the right sort of compliment
should be easy.

13 TUESDAY   *Moon Age Day 12   Moon Sign Taurus*

am . . . .

pm . . . .
The greatest successes at the moment are likely to come in terms of your
professional life and practical matters generally. Instead of insisting that
you should do your own thing, be willing to compromise, not a word
that occurs much in the Aries vocabulary. A day to look out for the odd
lucky break and use it to the full.

14 WEDNESDAY   *Moon Age Day 13   Moon Sign Taurus*

am . . . .

pm . . . .
If there are financial challenges around at the moment, these need to be
addressed very carefully. Perhaps you have been taking certain matters for
granted, but you won't be able to do so right now. Caution is the
keyword, something that is difficult for your zodiac sign to practise.

15 THURSDAY   *Moon Age Day 14   Moon Sign Gemini*

am . . . .

pm . . . .
Social matters and friendships especially could prove to be extremely
rewarding at this time. Even if you don't get through jobs quite as
quickly or easily as you had expected, you should get where you want to
be eventually. Happiness follows you throughout most of the day,
together with a feeling of contentment.

16 FRIDAY
Moon Age Day 15   Moon Sign Gemini

am . . . .

pm . . . .
The time is right to put domestic issues into focus, even if this means
ignoring some of the more practical issues of life for a while. Christmas
is just around the corner and you won't get away with shelving the issue.
Conforming to the patterns others set for you is probably easier than
would normally be the case.

17 SATURDAY
Moon Age Day 16   Moon Sign Cancer

am . . . .

pm . . . .
You still need to exercise a degree of caution when it comes to the
practical aspects of life, a fact that isn't made easier if so many demands
are now being made upon your time. It seems as though social
requirements are going off the scale so you may well have to spread
yourself very thinly.

18 SUNDAY
Moon Age Day 17   Moon Sign Cancer

am . . . .

pm . . . .
This is another period during which you could well have high spirits and
energy to spare. You find yourself in a good period to push for what you
want, even though some of the plans you are laying down will not mature
for another year or so. Combining your efforts with those who think the
way you do could prove to be sensible.

19 MONDAY
Moon Age Day 18   Moon Sign Leo

am . . . .

pm . . . .
Places of entertainment are now right up your street, which is probably just as well bearing in mind the time of year and the season. You can get by on very little when it comes to food and drink, so too much indulgence probably won't appeal to you around now. What you do relish is being in the social limelight.

20 TUESDAY
Moon Age Day 19   Moon Sign Leo

am . . . .

pm . . . .
The position of Venus in your chart brings a boost to friendships and enables you to make life-long pals out of some individuals who have only recently entered your sphere of influence. Social interactions generally prove to be highly rewarding, ahead of a slower phase as Christmas itself actually approaches.

21 WEDNESDAY
Moon Age Day 20   Moon Sign Virgo

am . . . .

pm . . . .
Life becomes even more interesting and there may be little time for circumspection. You find yourself to be very much a creature of the moment and won't have too many hours to spend meditating. Reacting in a moment-by-moment sense is what makes Aries tick, so such trends are no problem to you.

22 THURSDAY
Moon Age Day 21   Moon Sign Virgo

am . . . .

pm . . . .
You could meet with just the right sort of people today. They may even turn out to be not only individuals you like but also the right folk to include in your forward planning. Everything in your mind now has to be neat and organised, but don't be surprised if you are suddenly overtaken by a distinctly nostalgic frame of mind.

23 FRIDAY

Moon Age Day 22   Moon Sign Virgo

am . . . .

pm . . . .
Friendship-wise, a continuing influence shows itself whereby your world
becomes ever more pleasant and fulfilling. This is just as well, because
Christmas Day itself has some restrictions and bolstering yourself against
them now is worthwhile. A day to keep an open mind regarding the
peculiar behaviour of some family members.

24 SATURDAY

Moon Age Day 23   Moon Sign Libra

am . . . .

pm . . . .
It has to be said from the start that a relaxing Christmas Eve would suit
you best of all, thanks to the lunar low. For once you will be quite happy
to sit back and watch everyone else getting on with things. Family trends
are especially strong and some of the restless qualities of Aries are now
definitely shelved.

25 SUNDAY

Moon Age Day 24   Moon Sign Libra

am . . . .

pm . . . .
As Christmas Day arrives, you are still not too anxious to push yourself
forward or to live the high life. Those around you might be surprised at
your tendency to avoid too much drink or rich food. Still, you can be
content and happy with your lot and will be in a position to offer much
support to family members and friends.

26 MONDAY   *Moon Age Day 25   Moon Sign Scorpio*

am . . . .

pm . . . .
Airing the way you feel can sometimes be uncomfortable if you are an
Aries individual, though it is quite possible today. The position of the
Moon inclines you to spill the beans and you might become quite
emotional as a result. In the end, others should end up with a better
understanding of you.

27 TUESDAY   *Moon Age Day 26   Moon Sign Scorpio*

am . . . .

pm . . . .
Right now you find yourself much better off handling practical issues
alone. This doesn't mean you are isolating yourself but it does incline you
to being fairly independent. This is fine, just as long as you explain
yourself to others. It wouldn't be sensible to offer offence at a time when
help is also required.

28 WEDNESDAY   *Moon Age Day 27   Moon Sign Sagittarius*

am . . . .

pm . . . .
Social get-togethers ought to be positively affected by the presence of
Venus in your solar eleventh house. Even if you have been retreating
somewhat since Christmas, you are now likely to be back in the social
mainstream and should relish the company of interesting and
companionable types.

29 THURSDAY   *Moon Age Day 28   Moon Sign Sagittarius*

am . . . .

pm . . . .
Everyday obligations can now be a cause of some frustration. This
situation can be mitigated if you allow others to take some of the strain.
Delegating any facet of your life is not easy, but is a lesson worth learning
because it prevents you from becoming too fatigued. You would be wise
to avoid family arguments like the plague.

30 FRIDAY

Moon Age Day 0   Moon Sign Capricorn

am . . . .

pm . . . .
Freedom is the real key to happiness today. You find yourself involved in an upbeat and active period during which you are in a position to show your most positive face to the world at large. Your mind is exploring and the plans you are laying down for the year ahead reflect this fact all too well.

31 SATURDAY

Moon Age Day 1   Moon Sign Capricorn

am . . . .

pm . . . .
You will want to be noticed today and can afford to go to great lengths to make sure you are not ignored by anyone. Beware of alienating others by taking an attitude they can't understand. Your resolutions for the year ahead could well include a determination to push your practical capabilities to the full.

RISING SIGNS FOR ARIES

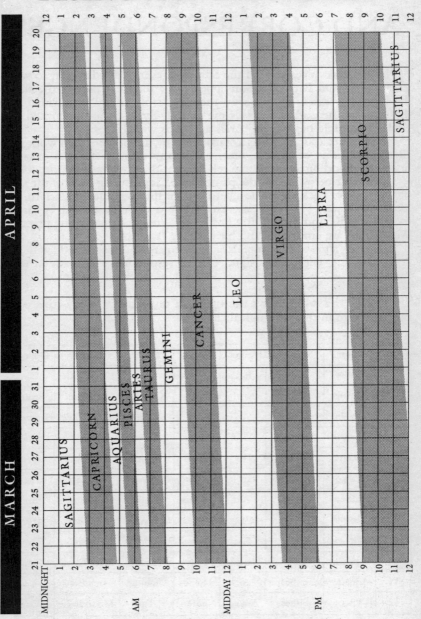

THE ZODIAC, PLANETS AND CORRESPONDENCES

The Earth revolves around the Sun once every calendar year, so when viewed from Earth the Sun appears in a different part of the sky as the year progresses. In astrology, these parts of the sky are divided into the signs of the zodiac and this means that the signs are organised in a circle. The circle begins with Aries and ends with Pisces.

Taking the zodiac sign as a starting point, astrologers then work with all the positions of planets, stars and many other factors to calculate horoscopes and birth charts and tell us what the stars have in store for us.

The table below shows the planets and Elements for each of the signs of the zodiac. Each sign belongs to one of the four Elements: Fire, Air, Earth or Water. Fire signs are creative and enthusiastic; Air signs are mentally active and thoughtful; Earth signs are constructive and practical; Water signs are emotional and have strong feelings.

It also shows the metals and gemstones associated with, or corresponding with, each sign. The correspondence is made when a metal or stone possesses properties that are held in common with a particular sign of the zodiac.

Finally, the table shows the opposite of each star sign – this is the opposite sign in the astrological circle.

Placed	Sign	Symbol	Element	Planet	Metal	Stone	Opposite
1	Aries	Ram	Fire	Mars	Iron	Bloodstone	Libra
2	Taurus	Bull	Earth	Venus	Copper	Sapphire	Scorpio
3	Gemini	Twins	Air	Mercury	Mercury	Tiger's Eye	Sagittarius
4	Cancer	Crab	Water	Moon	Silver	Pearl	Capricorn
5	Leo	Lion	Fire	Sun	Gold	Ruby	Aquarius
6	Virgo	Maiden	Earth	Mercury	Mercury	Sardonyx	Pisces
7	Libra	Scales	Air	Venus	Copper	Sapphire	Aries
8	Scorpio	Scorpion	Water	Pluto	Plutonium	Jasper	Taurus
9	Sagittarius	Archer	Fire	Jupiter	Tin	Topaz	Gemini
10	Capricorn	Goat	Earth	Saturn	Lead	Black Onyx	Cancer
11	Aquarius	Waterbearer	Air	Uranus	Uranium	Amethyst	Leo
12	Pisces	Fishes	Water	Neptune	Tin	Moonstone	Virgo

09068 229 723: *ring Old Moore now* – for the most authentic personal phone horoscope ever made available

Then just tap in your own birth date …

… and benefit from the wisdom of the centuries

The uncanny foresight of Britain's No1 astrologer – focused directly on your own individual *birth-chart*

Unique personalised reading

There's never been a better way to exploit your personal horoscope opportunities.

Old Moore now has a massive new computer with which he can produce a personal forecast based on the actual day of your birth. No other astro phone service can produce this level of accuracy.

Any day of the week, Old Moore can update you on the planetary influences which surround you and point up the opportunities which will be open to you.

Unique record of prediction

The principles of astro interpretation laid down by Old Moore three centuries ago have proved amazingly reliable and accurate right up to the present day. That's how the unique Old Moore system can be harnessed to analyse your own personal world.

Meet Old Moore any day

For just 60p per minute you can hear this authoritative overview of your life, work and happiness. Not the usual 'fortune-telling' patter, but enlightened insights into how best to exploit the day and the *immediate*.

Remember, unlike any other phone astrologer, Old Moore will ask you for the *day, month and year* of your birth, to give you the most individual advice and predictions ever possible.

So touch hands with the immortal Old Moore. Ring this number and get a truly personalised forecast, from the world's most acclaimed astrologer.

This service is only available on a touch tone button phone.

09068 229 723

Calls cost 60p per minute at all times.
(Charges may be higher for payphones and non-BT networks.)